Expectant

MOMENTS

DEVOTIONS
FOR EXPECTANT COUPLES

GENE & LISA FANT

ZondervanPublishingHouse
Grand Rapids, Michigan

A Division of HarperCollins*Publishers*

Expectant Moments
Copyright © 1999 by Gene Fant, Jr., and Lisa Fant

Requests for information should be addressed to:

ZondervanPublishingHouse
Grand Rapids, Michigan 49530

Library of Congress Cataloging-in-Publication Data

Fant, Gene C. (Gene Clinton), Jr.
    Expectant Moments : devotions for expectant couples / Gene and
Lisa Fant.
      p. cm.
      ISBN 0-310-22727-5
    1. Parents Prayer-books and devotions—English 2. Pregnancy
Prayer-books and devotions—English. I. Fant, Lisa, 1964– . II. Title.
BV4845.F35 1999
242'.645—dc21   99-31486
                                                  CIP

This edition printed on acid-free paper.

Interior design by Sherri Hoffman

Printed in the United States of America

---

99 00 01 02 03 04 05 /❖ DC/ 10 9 8 7 6 5 4 3 2 1

For our little ones, Ethan Edison and Emily Elisabeth

ACKNOWLEDGMENTS

We are overwhelmed by the love and understanding of our families and friends as they have supported us, prayed for us, and provided anecdotes for this project. You have made writing a book during pregnancy and early parenthood possible. Each of you knows that your prayers helped to give us children, and your prayers will help to raise our children. Thanks to our moms and dads for your sacrifices, and to Tina, especially, thanks for the diaper changes and the extra pair of arms.

To Drs. Jesse Ethridge, John Isaacs, Bryan Cowan, and your staffs. You encouraged us, advised us, and you were used by God to give us children. Truly, the miraculous and the medical work together.

To the entire English Department at Mississippi College, thanks for picking up the slack during our pregnancy and the process of writing. You epitomize Christian friendship and collegiality.

To Sandy Vander Zicht and the folks at Zondervan, your patience and insight have made it happen. Thanks for believing in our vision.

Finally, to our children, Ethan and Emily, you inspire us. We are truly blessed!

CONTENTS

INTRODUCTION

Bookstore shelves are filled with all kinds of pregnancy books: books on the medical facts of pregnancy, the foundations of parenting, even devotional books for expectant moms. However, when we went looking for a resource to help us prepare spiritually as a couple for this new stage in our family life, we could find none.

We knew how much we needed to use this special time to deal with the physical, emotional, and spiritual changes of pregnancy. Furthermore, we wanted to find a way to work through these issues as a couple, shoring up our marital relationship before our children arrived. Since we could find no resources to guide us in our journey, we decided to write one in the hope that other couples would find encouragement in our experiences.

Our vision has been for a devotional book, not a how-to manual for couples needing to work through serious problems. The devotions are meant to be used as "starters" for meditation, prayer, and discussion.

The book is divided into thirteen weeks (approximately one trimester), each week covering a different topic. You may read the devotionals in the order they come or skip around to whatever topic seems pertinent to you at the time. We suggest that you first read the extended Scripture passage listed, allowing God's Word to speak to your hearts before you focus on the devotional topic.

We pray that as you read the Scripture passages and devotional thoughts, talk about the issues presented, and pray, you will grow in unity as marriage partners, become better prepared parents, and mature in your faith.

1 Peter 2:2–3: Like newborn babies, crave pure spiritual milk, so that by it you may grow up in your salvation, now that you have tasted that the Lord is good.

EXPECTING

MOM'S THOUGHTS:
The Joy of Pregnancy

> LUKE 1:26–38,
> 46–56
> *And Mary said:*
> *"My soul glorifies the*
> *Lord and my spirit*
> *rejoices in God my*
> *Savior" (vv. 46–47).*

I couldn't wait any longer. I threw on my tennis shoes—no socks—drove to the pharmacy, and grabbed something I had wanted to purchase for a long time. With a lump in my throat and timidity in my spirit, I laid the pregnancy test on the counter, wondering if the woman at the checkout recognized the significance of my little purchase.

Back home, with shaky hands I followed the test directions carefully, then waited what seemed an interminable time for the reading. (I waited an extra minute, just to make sure.) My heart felt faint as I picked up the plastic stick and saw a dark purple line. *I'm pregnant!* I thought. *I'm pregnant!*

Robot-like, I walked to the den and asked Gene if he could come over to me for a minute.

"Is everything all right?" he asked.

I held out the stick, seeing the same numb shock in his eyes that I felt. Then I made him read the directions just to make sure I was interpreting them correctly.

Amazingly, we did not hug, laugh, or cry because neither one of us allowed ourselves to trust the home-test results. We had waited so long for this; our next wedding anniversary would be our ninth. We had prayed time after time for children; had seen numerous specialists; had read every imaginable piece of literature on infertility. Every month for the past several years had been a roller coaster of rising hope and sinking despair. We couldn't imagine all that coming to an end—so quickly—just by reading a few lines on a stick.

It wasn't until I saw my doctor the next morning that I allowed myself to start believing the truth. I was pregnant! The nurses hugged me and cried with me. By the time I reached the car, I was so full of emotion that the only appropriate outlet for my joy was singing. As I pondered the miracle that had occurred in my own life, I kept thinking of the words of Mary's song that I had memorized from a Christmas cantata. The miracle promised to Mary was of course the most special of all—she would give birth to the Son of God. However, I recognized the miraculous nature of what was occurring inside of me as well, and indeed my soul did praise the Lord.

Though I felt a little silly riding down the interstate singing at the top of my lungs, I knew that my response was pleasing to God. I sang wholeheartedly, "My soul doth magnify the Lord, my soul doth magnify the Lord, and my spirit doth rejoice in God my Savior."

Some time later, I received a congratulatory card from my Grandma Williams. In her letter, she told me she had been thinking of this same passage of Scripture describing Mary's joy. Through her encouraging words, God affirmed my act of worship.

What was your miracle moment like? How did you express your joy at finding out you were expecting? You may want to share some of your feelings with your spouse and take a moment together to praise the One who has given you this new life.

Lord, teach us to recognize the miracle moments of our lives, remembering to praise the One who has chosen us to share in the creation of life.

DAD'S THOUGHTS:

The Joy of Pregnancy

> **GENESIS 21:1–7**
> *Abraham was a hundred years old when his son Isaac was born to him. Sarah said, "God has brought me laughter, and everyone who hears about this will laugh with me. . . .*
> *Who would have said to Abraham that Sarah would nurse children?" (vv. 5–7).*

One of our favorite episodes of *I Love Lucy* is when Lucy tries to tell the busy, unsuspecting Ricky that after so many years of marriage, they are going to have a baby. Her repeated efforts to tell him the news are thwarted at every turn until Ricky finally figures out what's going on. The sweet closing scene shows Lucy and Ricky sharing a tender embrace before fading into the famous heart outline that ends each episode.

I was working in my office when Lisa (after her visit to her doctor for an official pregnancy test) knocked on my door, poked her head in, and asked, "Do you want to be a dad?"

I had been in on the results of the home pregnancy test, so I knew why she had seen the doctor that morning. But on actually hearing that I, at long last—after all those years of trying—was going to be a father . . . my reaction was a mixture of surprise, excitement, and fear.

What must Abraham and Sarah have felt when they began to realize that she was pregnant at her age? Imagine those two senior citizens going through pregnancy and all the work of a newborn baby! When little Isaac became colicky or cranky, did Sarah continue to think about her joy at having a little one of her own? Perhaps, as she washed out those dirty diapers or whatever they used back then, she even praised God.

We finally were going to have a baby! I realize that we will be worn out, exhausted after the little one arrives. Everyone keeps telling me that my life will never be the same again. I don't understand exactly what they mean by that comment, but I'm reasonably certain that they are right. I just hope I will never forget the joy that the baby, even before it is born, has already brought us.

> *God, help us never to lose our wonder at your work in our lives and in your blessing us with our little one.*

STANDING IN AWE OF GOD

ISAIAH 29:22–24
*When they see among
them their children,
the work of my
hands, they will keep
my name holy; they
will acknowledge the
holiness of the Holy
One of Jacob, and
will stand in awe of
the God of Israel
(v. 23).*

Lisa has just begun to feel the movements of the babies. What an exciting time we have had, trying to figure out their positions, which parts are moving, and what triggers the babies' wiggling. We are amazed at just how active those little ones are. Friends have told us that late in the pregnancy, the kicks of their babies were so strong they could see the outline of an actual foot!

At a Christmas concert the other night, Lisa glanced over at me with a startled look as everyone in the audience stood for the "Hallelujah Chorus." One baby seemed to be dancing in response to the music, and the other seemed to be standing right on top of her bladder! While her look meant that this was uncomfortable, I, the proud papa-to-be, was busy thinking about how smart that child was already to know when to stand out of respect for the Messiah.

How rarely do we stand in awe of God! We know his greatness and his goodness, but often we fail to recognize his absolute splendor. Think for a moment about his majesty, his holiness, his love; does your heart stir as you ponder these things? In our harried lives, we often take God for granted, forgetting to reflect on him.

We want to teach our little ones to respect the Lord in all ways and to recognize his majesty. We pray that they will accept his lordship over their lives and will dedicate their lives to serving him. We also desire to be examples to our children of how much we should respect God and stand in awe of his presence.

God, we stand in awe of you. Give us and our little ones a glimpse of your glory.

SURPRISES

ROMANS
11:33–36

Oh, the depth of the riches of the wisdom and knowledge of God! How unsearchable his judgments, and his paths beyond tracing out! Who has known the mind of the Lord? Or who has been his counselor? Who has ever given to God, that God should repay him? For from him and through him and to him are all things. To him be the glory forever! Amen.

What a phone call it was. A nurse at Lisa's doctor's office called to ask Lisa to make an appointment for an ultrasound. The blood test confirming our pregnancy, she explained, had indicated unusually high hormone levels. The high levels were still there on a second test. Even though we were only about seven weeks into the pregnancy, the doctor wanted to do an ultrasound to check things out.

High hormone levels, we had heard, could signal any number of conditions, including some forms of mental retardation and multiple babies in the womb, so we began to brace ourselves for whatever would be discovered. Frankly, we were nervous. Our joy with the pregnancy was now tinged by the uncertainties of pregnancy.

The day of the ultrasound, a technician, a nurse, and the doctor came into the examination room. Lisa was already on the table. Someone dimmed the lights. All eyes went to the black-and-white images on the screen as the doctor, holding the ultrasound wand, began to search over Lisa's womb. Soon a little black blob appeared, and the doctor stopped moving the wand. He zoomed in, enlarging that one area, then pointed to a little white lump within the dark region.

"That's the baby," he said, adding, as he made some notes, "That one looks good."

For some reason the way he said "that one" made us nervous, and we looked at each other as he began to move the wand around some more.

"Ah, ha! Here's the other one." He paused.

"I thought so," said the nurse who had called us to make the appointment.

"Are you sure it's *only* two?" I asked. "Please make sure!"

The doctor double-checked. "Two. Twins."

Twins! I squeezed Lisa's hand. She look up at me and smiled.

Somewhere in heaven my Granny Irene must have grabbed her twin sister Maxine and yelled down at us, "Hooray! When you two got married, I told you this would happen. You should have listened to your granny!"

Lisa and I found ourselves asking all sorts of questions: *Why would God entrust two babies to us? How can Lisa, as little as she is, carry two babies at the same time? God, are you sure that you know what you're doing?*

Now, as we think back on our thoughts in that moment, we realize that we were actually questioning God's wisdom. What a silly and pride-filled endeavor to think that we know better than the Lord of the universe! As the pregnancy has progressed, we find ourselves constantly amazed at God's wisdom, his providence, and his love. Paul reminds us that

God knows more than we do, and, therefore, we can trust in his wisdom. No matter what surprises might lie ahead, God loves us and cares for us. He is faithful, even in these days of uncertainty.

> *God, prepare us for what surprises may be hidden in the days ahead. Remind us that your wisdom will always sustain us, even in the uncertainties of life.*

IN DUE TIME

LUKE 2:25–38
*She never left the temple
but worshiped night
and day, fasting and
praying. Coming up to
them at that very
moment, she gave
thanks to God and
spoke about the child
to all who were looking
forward to the redemp-
tion of Jerusalem
(vv. 37–38).*

"You'll never guess the due date for the babies," Lisa said one day on her return from the doctor's office. "April 23."

"You're kidding," I said. "April 23?"

For two English teachers, April 23 is one of the most significant dates in literary history, for it is the feast date of Saint George (the patron saint of England), the date Shakespeare was born, and the date that Shakespeare and Cervantes (the author of *Don Quixote*) died. How ironic that our children's due date falls on that particular date.

I pulled out my day planner and wrote "BABIES" on the date, surrounding it with stars. Lisa took down the calendar we keep in the kitchen and wrote "DUE DATE" in large red letters. We made the cycle through the phone list of relatives and told each of them to mark the date on their calendars. Over the next few months every occurrence in our lives would be measured by its proximity to that date. Spring break, five weeks before the due date. Easter, just two weeks before. Final exams, two weeks after.

Every time we think about that date marked on the calendar we get excited with expectation, realizing how soon our children will be here! We can hardly contain our joy at the prospect of seeing our own children face-to-face.

When Simeon and Anna discovered that they would see their Savior face-to-face, they spent their days rejoicing and worshiping God, right up until the day when Joseph and Mary brought Jesus to the temple for his dedication. Their hopeful expectation was great, but not as great as the joy they felt on that day.

We feel that same expectation regarding our children. As we think about our joy over their coming, we are reminded about the even greater joy we should have in knowing that the Christ child has already come and has brought salvation into the world. Now we understand even better the joyous expectation that accompanied Christ's birth.

How hard it must have been for Simeon and Anna to have been patient as they waited. We are impatient already, but we know that for the babies to be healthy, the proper amount of time must pass. Our children will come in due time, just as the Christ child came in the fullness of time. God grants us joyous patience, and we realize that his promises come to fulfillment at the proper time, in the proper season. We must await his timing with praise, excitement, and patience.

God, we thank you for the birth of our Savior, and we thank you for the expectation we now have over the birth of our children. Make us patient as we wait, and make us joyous in our expectation.

SHARING THE NEWS

> **PROVERBS**
> **15:30**
> *A cheerful look brings joy to the heart, and good news gives health to the bones.*

One of the happiest times in this pregnancy has been when we shared the news with our family and friends. When we finished telling everyone, we had to call them all back later to tell them that we were having twins! We tried to think of creative ways to tell them about the twins. When we called Gene's parents, he asked his dad if he wanted to be a grandpa.

"Of course," Dad Fant said. "I told you yes two weeks ago!"

"Dad, I'm asking you a second time, do you want to be a grandpa?"

"Well, of course . . . wait a minute, why are you asking me *twice?* Is it twins? Your granny was right all those years ago!"

Boy, did we have a huge phone bill that month! Telling parents that they are going to be grandparents, sisters and brothers that they will be aunts and uncles, and extended family that another little one will be running around at Christmas get-togethers is one of the great joys of life.

Being the bearer of good news is always fun. We have good news about the birth of another baby: Jesus. How much fun the angels must have had announcing the news to the shepherds in the field. Likewise, the disciples must have been bursting with gladness as they shared the news of the

Resurrection. The good news of God's love to humankind and Christ's redemptive work can bring great joy and spiritual health to those who hear it. How wonderful that we can still share that joyous news today.

God, thank you for giving us the opportunity to experience the joy of sharing the good news of our pregnancy. Help us to capture that same joy when we tell others of the baby in the manger.

A WOMB WITH A VIEW

That first sonogram of the babies continues to amaze us. The doctor's printed screen captured the images, and we have made copies for everyone in the family. Our parents have taped them to their refrigerators—our children's first portraits. At seven weeks the little amniotic sacs of our twins form a tiny figure eight. Though they are only about an inch or so long, we can make out their heads, hearts, and even their tiny limb buds, especially their legs.

Our parents are amazed to see that the babies are so recognizable at such an early date. When they were expecting us, they did not have such easy access to resources showing exactly what the little ones looked like on a week-by-week basis. I enlarged a copy of the sonogram and taped it to my office door, complete with a diagram explaining what everything was. My students are just as amazed as my parents. How remarkable technology is, giving us a peek at our children so early in their lives.

We can't help but think of David's wonderful psalm about God's care for children while yet they lie in their mothers' wombs. They are being "knit" into persons who are "fearfully and wonderfully made." David didn't have the technology to see this process of development, but he understood the wonder of the Creator's intimate knowledge of us as individuals.

While our babies are yet in the womb, he already loves and cares for them.

> God, thank you for watching over our little ones as they grow. Help us to remember their miraculous status as creations in the image of God.

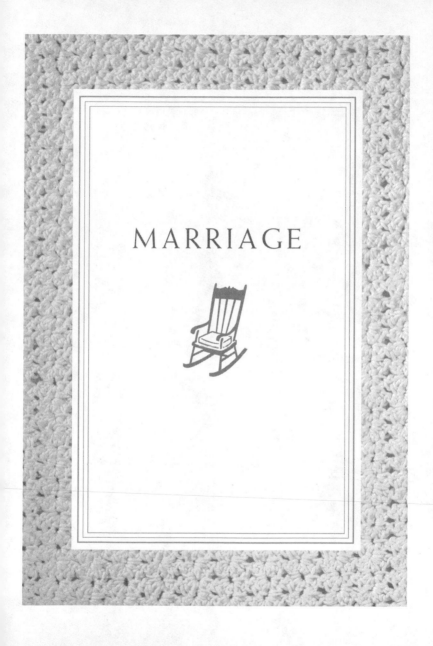

MARRIAGE

DON'T FORGET TO SHARE

> GENESIS 2:20–24
> *The man said, "This is now bone of my bones and flesh of my flesh; she shall be called 'woman,' for she was taken out of man." For this reason a man will leave his father and mother and be united to his wife, and they will become one flesh (vv. 23–24).*

Before Kathy and Steve had a chance to tell anyone that they were pregnant, they received news that Steve's grandfather had died. Although his death had been expected, Steve and Kathy decided this wasn't the best time to tell family members their good news, so they decided to wait. Although it was difficult to keep the secret, it was also a blessing to share this knowledge with only each other. No one else knew this incredibly personal, wonderful secret but them. It was like the quiet before the storm—before all the excitement and congratulations, before the planning and the preparations—a private moment of bliss and oneness.

Having children is the ultimate expression of oneness in marriage. Ideally, pregnancy is a physical manifestation of a couple's physical, intellectual, and spiritual union. Pregnancy can be a time to develop the sense of oneness so real to you right now, or pregnancy can alienate you from each other. Whether you end up closer to, or farther from, the wholeness God intended for married couples depends on how well you share the experiences of life. So, how do you allow pregnancy to unify you when so many factors (body changes, money, time constraints) are working to pull you apart? How do you share the pregnancy? Obviously, men cannot participate in everything pregnant women are going through, nor can women experience what it is like to become fathers, but spouses can show interest and empathy in what is going on with their partner.

Going to obstetrician appointments together has allowed us to share some tender moments. Gene has not been able to make all of the appointments, but he goes to as many as he can. I try to schedule them at times when he can adjust his work schedule. Not only does this arrangement give us time to chat on the forty-minute drive to and from the doctor's office, but it allows Gene to participate in hearing the babies' heartbeats and seeing them on the sonograms. He gets to ask his own questions and interpret the doctor's comments. We always have lots to talk about on the way home from these visits and often squeeze in a mini-date, stopping at a fast-food place for a soft drink or a bacon, egg, and cheese biscuit (which I crave). Obviously, not all couples have flexible work schedules, but when you make something a priority, you can often find ways to do it.

Reading about pregnancy, fetal development, and birth has also provided opportunities for sharing. Since this is our first pregnancy, we have especially enjoyed looking at one magazine that contains color photos of the growing child in the womb, month-by-month, from conception to birth. We lie in bed at night and wonder at our very own growing miracles, knowing that they look somewhat like these amazing photographs.

Attending childbirth classes together also gives us shared experiences. Although we have a wonderful childbirth educator who creates a comfortable atmosphere for the class, we have still felt a little silly practicing massage and breathing techniques in a room full of people. Gene just can't take it seriously. But sharing the experience at least has given us a private joke to chuckle about later.

Some of these experiences may not work for you, and if this pregnancy is not your first, you may find it more difficult to find the time for or to get excited about all of these activities. Whatever your circumstance, you can commit to sharing in ways that work for you as a couple. Some men are really uncomfortable with too much candor about the physical realities of pregnancy and birth. If you're in this group, you should discuss boundary lines with your wife as well as other limitations such as time, work schedules, and the schedules of your other children. It's important to discuss possible means of working around these.

Lord, use our pregnancy to strengthen our unity. Help us to learn from each other as we go through this time together.

TEAMWORK

PHILIPPIANS
2:1–5
*If you have any
encouragement from
being united with
Christ, if any comfort
from his love, if any
fellowship with the
Spirit, if any tender-
ness and compassion,
then make my joy
complete by being
like-minded, having
the same love, being
one in spirit and pur-
pose (vv. 1–2).*

When we began to renovate our house, we discovered that we didn't work together very well. For example, we both had definite ideas about how the painting should be done. Lisa, following the example of her fix-it dad, wanted to prevent spills by using an overabundance of tape, newspaper, and plastic drop cloths, while I would rather clean up minor messes after the painting is done. Lisa wanted to start early and be done before supper; I wanted to sleep in, start after lunch, and work into the evening. We disagreed over when the trim work should be painted and who would paint it, over what kind of rollers and paintbrushes to buy, and over what color paint to use.

We had several choices. We could hire the work done, which was out of the question with our budget. Lisa could do the work herself, but she lacked the muscle for the overhead painting that the cathedral ceilings would require. I could do all the work, but the time demands of my job made that impossible. We could leave the work half done (not a satisfactory resolution for either of us). Or we could learn to work together, keeping our goal in mind.

We chose the latter, and an amazing process occurred. We became better at talking about our ideas, compromising when necessary, and dividing jobs according to who did what best. Since Lisa was more detail-oriented, she picked out (with my approval) colors that anticipated the other changes we would be making in the house, and she prepared the rooms for painting by taping and covering areas that would not be painted; she painted much of the trim several days before the walls were painted. I purchased the supplies, removed doors and hardware, and painted the large areas that required a roller and some muscle. Soon we were working like a well-oiled machine. We painted four rooms and a hallway but, more important, we increased the unity in our marriage.

Working on our house was a good warm-up for pregnancy and parenting. The preparations for welcoming a little one into the world can be a real test of a couple's decision-making skills. We must decide which car seat is best, whether to breast-feed or bottle-feed, which immunizations we want our babies to have, how much life insurance to buy, whether or not to have the umbilical cord blood stored, and whether to have our son circumcised. If we make it through all of the decisions surrounding pregnancy and birth, we will move on to the real test of marital unity: raising children together. Like most parents-to-be, we are a little unsure of our ability to navigate all of these decisions while preserving and increasing our unity as a couple.

On the cover of our wedding program is a drawing of a wedding cross. This symbol shows two wedding rings intertwined with a cross—a visual representation of the message of Philippians 2.

The foundation for unity with your spouse is a life that exists in true unity with Christ. Because we are unified with Christ, we experience encouragement, comfort, fellowship, tenderness, and compassion. Because we are healed, whole, loved, and complete in him, we are at liberty to stop competing with our spouse, to stop protecting our egos, and to start compromising in the name of achieving oneness with our partner. Growing together as a couple is still possible— even with children—if we remember that through Christ we are one in spirit and in purpose.

Lord, thank you for our unity with Christ. Thank you for how that unity enables us to find fellowship with others, especially our spouse.

CHANGING ROLES AND RESPONSIBILITIES

1 PETER 3:7
Husbands, in the same way be considerate as you live with your wives, and treat them with respect as the weaker partner and as heirs with you of the gracious gift of life, so that nothing will hinder your prayers.

A bag of cat litter taught me this lesson: an expectant mother cannot do everything she once did. At seven months, my weekly shopping excursion had become a wearying task. Gene had offered to take over this chore, but I was reluctant to relinquish any job that got me out of the house. Besides, we were on a tight budget, and I was a good bargain shopper. Shopping was my job, and I took pride in doing it well.

On this particular trip, I already had been in the store for an hour and a half. Exhausted, I headed for the cat litter, the last item on my long list. As I reached down to pull up the 25-pound bag from a low shelf, I realized I couldn't lift it and, even if I could, wisdom would discourage such an action at this stage of the pregnancy. I looked around and could find no one to help me. I considered getting a smaller bag, but my penny-pincher pride just wouldn't let me commit such an extravagance.

I finally spotted a clerk helping a mother and her little girl net a goldfish—the girl's first goldfish, I gathered from their conversation.

"Is this one okay, honey?" asked the clerk hopefully. The girl stood on her tiptoes to see the trapped goldfish, and then she looked at her weary mother.

Cute, I thought. *One day, I'll be doing that with my little girl, but right now I'm too tired to savor this Kodak moment. This could take forever.* There were no other clerks in sight, so I inched a little closer, trying politely to make my presence known.

A long pause followed. My back was killing me. My favorite tennis shoes were no longer cushioning the effects of the concrete floor on my swollen feet. I was so tired. I wanted to sit right down in the middle of the aisle, but I knew I'd never be able to get up—at least not without help, and help seemed to be a long wait away.

"Okay," said the girl tentatively.

The clerk looked relieved.

I moved a little closer and sighed impatiently. I considered leaving without the kitty litter but figured I had waited this long, why not persevere to the end. Finally, fifteen minutes from the moment I had first sought help, the clerk hoisted my cat litter onto my shopping cart. As the bag hit the cart, I realized to my utter dismay that I would have to go through this ordeal again to get the bag in my car! When I arrived home, completely exhausted, we decided Gene would take over the weekly shopping from that point on.

God created a partnership in marriage that works when we get out of the way. During pregnancy, jobs can no longer be "his" or "hers," "yours" or "mine." Husbands may need to take on more responsibilities as the due date approaches, particularly in high-risk pregnancies or when other young children are present. Just as Christ washed his disciples' feet, a husband may find himself washing his toddlers' feet or at least rubbing his wife's swollen ankles.

Roles and responsibilities are often points of conflict in marriage. Do you remember having arguments when you were first married over who was going to do the dishes? Just when you think you've finally worked out who will take out the trash and clean the toilets and cook the dinner, pregnancy turns those comfortable roles upside down, necessitating that couples start from scratch, talking over responsibilities, adapting, and adjusting until the baby comes—and afterwards.

This role shifting might make both of you feel uncomfortable. After all, our roles and how well we fill them contribute to our self-esteem. I was hesitant to give up my "job" as official family shopper. I traded that responsibility for one that was physically less taxing—balancing the checkbook. The trade-off helped ease Gene's already overburdened workload. The two of us reached a mutually beneficial agreement, thereby contributing to our unity as marriage partners. Isn't unity the goal of marriage?

God, help us to settle any areas of conflict over our roles and responsibilities. Teach us to be considerate of each other.

MAKING TIME FOR MARRIAGE

> **DEUTERONOMY 24:5**
>
> *If a man has recently married, he must not be sent to war or have any other duty laid on him. For one year he is to be free to stay at home and bring happiness to the wife he has married.*

On any other Sunday, Lisa would have stuck the marriage conference brochure into her Bible only to be found six months later with the old church bulletins stashed between 2 Kings and 1 Chronicles. On this particular day, however, she pulled out the flyer on the way home from church to ask me if I would like to attend.

We had never been to a marriage conference. We had never had the time or the money, and besides, our marriage was in good shape. Why bother with some touchy-feely conference to work on a marriage that was just fine? As we discussed the possibility of attending, we realized nothing had changed: we were busier and had less disposable income than ever; we felt our marriage was strong; and Lisa, in addition, dreaded the thought of sitting through a lengthy conference with the weight of twins pushing on her back and bladder. So we can't really say why we decided to go, but we did.

In spite of our hesitancy, God used that conference to strengthen our marriage. He rewarded our commitment to set aside time for marriage. The point of the Deuteronomy passage is not that we should get a year's paid vacation to honeymoon (shucks!) but that new marriages require time. We can always find reasons to avoid spending time doing the hard work of marriage building. During pregnancy, we can fall into the trap of neglecting our relationship because we are so completely baby-centered; however, a child-centered family is not a healthy family. If we ignore our relationship with each other, we will be robbing not only ourselves but also our children of the family life God intends.

When was the last time you set aside time to work on your marriage? Although you may not be able to go to a marriage conference, you might find other ways to make time for your marriage, like planning a brief getaway or working through a marriage book together.

Father, may we never take for granted the blessing of marriage. Renew our resolve to commit time and energy to strengthening our marriage so that our children will reap the benefits.

IT'S THE LITTLE THINGS THAT MATTER

> **1 JOHN 3:18**
> *Dear children, let us not love with words or tongue but with actions and in truth.*

"Love" is a word that's thrown around so often that we hardly know what it means. I *love* homemade ice cream. I *love* golf. I *love* my dog. How can your spouse know that you love her more than you love the dog? By your actions. The phone calls in the middle of the day, the words of praise you use in the company of friends, the surprise kisses, the notes tucked into a briefcase all add up to a big fat "I love you more than ice cream and more than the dog. In fact, I love you more than life itself."

The context for 1 John 3:18 is Christ's laying down his life for us (v. 16). Christ's act, states John, is the very definition of love. Rarely are we called upon to give up our physical lives for each other. Rather, we pour out ourselves little by little; we lay down our lives every day in the little things we do or don't do.

Pregnancy provides so many new opportunities to do nice things for each other: the day we find out that Lisa is pregnant, the day we find out the sex of the baby, the day we first hear the heartbeat or feel the baby kick, the day of Lisa's first craving for pistachio ice cream. All of these milestones are great excuses for little gestures that commemorate the occasion. For example, to welcome his wife and baby girl home from the hospital, my brother, Steve, decorated their mailbox with balloons. The benefits of this one small action are multiplied every time his wife, Kathy, watches the video-tape of their homecoming. That little gesture paid big dividends in marital unity! The little acts of kindness, the demonstrations of affection are the memorable markers that turn our mundane lives into fulfilling ones.

Pregnancy can reawaken some of those warm, fuzzy, goose-pimply feelings we had when we first met—the kind of feelings that make us do things without needing a special occasion. Take advantage of these feelings as reminders to do some of the foolish little things you did when you were courting.

When we were first dating, I would pick wildflowers and put them under the windshield wiper blades of Lisa's car. I loved driving halfway across the county to sneak them to her, and she loved finding them as she left work. I still like to grab a $4.99 bouquet at the grocery store from time to time, and I find myself doing it more often since Lisa became pregnant. Her usual response is, "What's the occasion?" I think she knows the answer to that question, but she likes to hear my reply, "Just because I love you!"

Hokey? Maybe, but Proverbs 5:18 reminds me to rejoice in the wife of my youth. I love to remember those days when my youthful blood would surge at the very thought of her. Those flowers make me feel young as much as they make Lisa feel loved—a mutually beneficial deal!

Perhaps flowers and candy aren't your style, but you can talk about some of the little things you've done for each other in the past. You may want to relive those loving moments as well as think about what you might do to commemorate some of the milestones of pregnancy.

Father, teach us to love not just in words but in kind actions. Make us sensitive to specific actions that make each other feel loved. Teach us to be creative in our kindnesses.

NAVEL GAZING

MATTHEW
22:39
*"Love your neighbor
as yourself."*

Jim had been up late working on the nursery and preparing for a big presentation at work. He was already running late and was searching desperately in his closet for a shirt. *They must still be in the dryer,* he thought. Sure enough, Jim found a miserably wrinkled shirt in the cold dryer. He quickly set up the ironing board, plugged in the iron, and went to the kitchen to grab something to eat. He sniffed the milk carton, "Whew!" He poured the soured milk, which was a week past the expiration date, down the sink. In the pantry, he found a stale Pop-Tart that he ate while he ironed his shirt and went over the outline for his presentation.

"Honey, can you tie my shoes? I can't reach my feet," came Carol's voice from the bedroom.

"Sure, Sweetie. Be right there." Jim threw on his shirt, draped his tie around his neck, and met Carol in the dining room where, eight-and-a-half months pregnant, she plopped on a chair, foot extended.

"You know, we *must* finish the nursery tonight. I feel like I could have this baby at any minute. Did you know that his lungs are fully developed now? He could be born anytime and be just fine. At least I've got everything packed except for my toothbrush. I hope I don't forget my toothbrush, and I just need to buy diaper ointment and nail clippers for the

nursery. Oh, and a night-light. Can't forget the night-light."
Her voice trailed off as she made a mental note to buy the
night-light.

Jim finished the shoe, gave Carol a kiss, and began to fix
his tie.

"Thanks, Hon. Do these shoes make my feet look big?"

Without waiting for an answer, Carol continued,
"Remember, I've got a baby shower today, so I'll be late. Oh,
by the way, could you pick up my dry cleaning on the way
home since you go right by there?"

Jim started to remind Carol that he was supposed to go
to a football game with his buddy Mac that night, but he
thought better of it. Mac would understand, what with the
baby coming and all. "Hey, I can pick up dinner, too," Jim
added.

Jim grabbed his briefcase and kissed Carol, who was
dreamily admiring and folding some baby clothes she had
washed.

"Pray for me today, I've got this big pre—"

"Aren't they just adorable?" interrupted Carol, holding up
a miniature pair of socks.

"Adorable," agreed Jim. "I love you. Gotta go." Jim closed
the door behind him.

I have to admit that I, like Carol, have fallen into the trap
of dwelling on the belly—navel gazing, if you will. I can't see
much else in my world right now except my growing tummy
full of babies, and I'm sure Gene is feeling a little neglected.
Naturally, a pregnant woman will become more and more
baby-centered as the time for delivery approaches, but my
pregnancy cannot be an excuse for being self-centered. Jesus'

commandment is to love my neighbor, starting with my closest neighbor, my husband. I'm to love him as I love myself, and I must admit I'm pretty pleased with this self of mine that's doing such a good job of growing new little selves. It's all so fascinating and wonderful. Only the power of love, God's love, can help me put my preoccupations aside to recognize and to meet my husband's needs.

Lord, forgive me when I take my spouse for granted. Turn my eyes away from myself and toward my neighbors, starting with my spouse.

SHARING A BED

1 CORINTHIANS 7:3–5

The husband should fulfill his marital duty to his wife, and likewise the wife to her husband. The wife's body does not belong to her alone but also to her husband. In the same way, the husband's body does not belong to him alone but also to his wife. Do not deprive each other except by mutual consent and for a time, so that you may devote yourselves to prayer. Then come together again so that Satan will not tempt you because of your lack of self-control.

When we were first married, we slept like giant human spoons on about two feet of space on the mattress. It was amazing how neatly our bodies fit together, like complementary halves made for each other. We actually enjoyed sleeping and living closely (which was a blessing since our apartment had only 400 square feet of living space). Now, with the pregnancy, we have a queen-sized mattress because Lisa was feeling like she was rolling out of the bed, and I was feeling like I should be sleeping on the floor. In addition, Lisa builds a nest of pillows every night to support her tummy, her back, her legs, and her head.

Our sleeping arrangement is just a physical reminder of how our babies have already begun to change our relationship in a very literal sense: we just can't fit together quite like we once did. We suspect that this intervention may be only the beginning of disrupted marital sleeping habits!

The physical and emotional changes of pregnancy create new challenges for physical intimacy as well as for sleeping. Increases or decreases in a woman's sex drive, nausea, fatigue, fears about hurting or disturbing the baby, and changes in body shape affect a couple's sex life during pregnancy. Viewing these obstacles as opportunities to work together rather than as hindrances can add vitality to the physical relationship. New challenges are new chances for discussion, experimentation, and change. Having accurate medical information about what is "normal" can prepare us and ease some of our anxieties, but talking and praying together are keys to making it through pregnancy with our sex life intact. Although our relationship is changing, God's plan is still for us to experience physical, emotional, and spiritual oneness.

Lord, thank you for the gift of sex. Guide us as we work through the changes of pregnancy. Bring us closer to your ideal of oneness in all areas of our marriage.

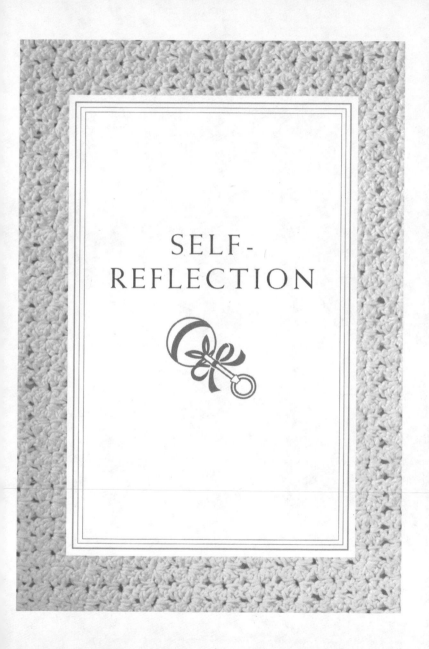

SELF-
REFLECTION

REFLECTING ON ADULTHOOD

> ## 1 CORINTHIANS 13:9–13
> *When I was a child, I talked like a child, I thought like a child, I reasoned like a child. When I became a man, I put childish ways behind me (v. 11).*

The other day I was visiting with one of my childhood buddies whose wife is expecting their first child. We were going down the checklist of our adult accomplishments, feeling a lot like one of those statistics on the suburban American dream: high school (check), college (check), career (check), marriage (check), house (check), and now kids (check). We are real adults who have traded our sports coupes for minivans and our blue jeans for khakis. We may have been able to fake our extended adolescence for a while before we had kids, but those baby seats in the back of the car are dead giveaways that we have become real adults. Certainly, there are other milestones ahead of us besides retirement and death!

Contrary to what television advertisements tell us, becoming an adult doesn't mean starting a slow death; rather, it means that we are maturing and growing. In our youth-oriented culture, it's hard to remember that growing older is not an affliction, that maturity and experience are rewards for which we work hard in life. When our little ones arrive, we will worry if they don't grow. The same still applies to us. Pregnancy is a good time to stand up next to our own growth charts and measure our maturity levels. Do we still have a few childish ways that we need to put behind us? Do we have issues resulting from past experiences that we need to put behind us? Perhaps we need to work on our self-discipline, personal ethics, or attitudes toward work; perhaps we need to tame our tongues or control our tempers.

If recent soul-searching has uprooted some areas where your personal growth is stunted, dedicate yourself now to completing the passage from extended adolescence into responsible adulthood.

Lord, teach us to embrace adulthood—its responsibilities and privileges. Reveal to us the areas where we need to work on our maturity.

REFLECTING ON THE PAST

> ISAIAH 43:18
> *Forget the former things; do not dwell on the past.*

When I was about seven, my mom found some lollipops hidden in my pillowcase. It didn't take long for her to confront me. "Where did you get these lollipops?"

"I got them at the store," I replied.

"With what money?"

"They were free. I didn't get charged nothing for them."

Of course, she knew what had happened—I had grabbed them and put them in my pocket. The candy counter in the store was between the cash register and the doorway. Customers passed the counter after they had paid their bills, so I reasoned (with the logic of a sweet-toothed child) that the candy must have been free. I have always sworn that I didn't know what I had done was wrong, but looking back now, I must have sensed the criminal nature of my actions or I wouldn't have hidden them in my room. To make amends, my parents had me write a note of apology to the store manager and send in payment (taken from an advance in my allowance) for the stolen lollipops. As a consequence for my behavior, they grounded me as well.

Because of my parents' wise discipline, I was truly contrite and never shoplifted again. In spite of the fact that I had made amends and been forgiven, however, those lollipops continued to haunt me even into my teen years. As slight as the incident may seem now, the memory of my past misdeed mocked me and made me feel sinful; I just couldn't clear my conscience of the shame. I finally began to pray that God would help me to put my transgression behind me and to forgive myself as he had already forgiven me.

The anticipation of having children causes us to reflect on our own childhoods. The guilt of past sins or even the shame of childhood victimizations may resurface. While dealing with the hurts of the past is important to our emotional well-being, dwelling on the past is useless and distracts us. The passage into parenthood is a good time to come to terms with our past, confessing old sins and hurts and embracing God's love and forgiveness. The clear message of the cross is that Christ has provided a future for us through *his* action in the past. We can live victoriously knowing that the past has passed.

Father, lift the burdens of the past from our shoulders. Give us the courage to fix our gazes upon your glory and the hope you provide.

REFLECTIONS ON MY INDIVIDUALITY

MATTHEW
10:29–31

Are not two sparrows sold for a penny? Yet not one of them will fall to the ground apart from the will of your Father. And even the very hairs of your head are all numbered. So don't be afraid; you are worth more than many sparrows.

I've noticed something lately; I am invisible. Actually, people do ask me questions, but never about *me*. How's Lisa? How are the babies? When is she due? What sex are they? What names have you picked out? My students don't look at me when they are in my office for conferences; they look at the sonograms on the door and over my desk. My roles as teacher, friend, even husband have been overshadowed by my new role as the expectant father of twins.

Both the expectant mom and dad may feel a little lost in their new roles as parents. The tendency is to slip into that role that equates us with the raising of our children. We tend to live our dreams through our little ones and set calendars by the children's activities, ignoring ourselves in the process. When we do that, we quickly find that we have no friends apart from our children, no personal interests, and very little marriage left by the time our nest is empty.

But becoming parents doesn't mean that we must lose our self-identities. More important than our role as parents is our status as beloved children of God. God sees every part of us, not just the parental part. Jesus referred us to the sparrows. They are almost invisible in our world; no one pays them much attention, but each one of them is valuable in God's eyes. How much more valuable are we, even when we feel invisible behind our role as parent.

Father, remind us of our value in your sight. Don't allow us to lose ourselves in our busy roles as parents.

REFLECTING ON MY WORDS

JAMES 3:3–12

All kinds of animals, birds, reptiles and creatures of the sea are being tamed and have been tamed by man, but no man can tame the tongue. It is a restless evil, full of deadly poison (vv. 7–8).

Children love wordplay. They will repeat words over and over, fascinated by the feel of them on their tongues and in their mouths. Dr. Seuss made a fortune off of children's natural enjoyment of silly sounding, nonsensical phrases and poems. Indeed, there are quite a few parents who have been embarrassed by their children's mimicking their words without knowing the meaning of what was being said.

So, have you started watching your words? We have. We are developing a radar for what is inappropriate for the sensitive ears of children. For example, Lisa will stop herself mid-sentence sometimes and say, "Oops, gotta stop talking like that!" I have the bad habit of using sarcasm, and from time to time my love for puns and wit drives me over the line of good taste. Although Lisa has learned not to take it personally, when we were first married my flippant sarcasm used to hurt her feelings.

Did you know that "sarcasm" actually means "cutting of flesh"? We certainly don't want to use words that wound our children's tender spirits. Words are more than meaningless sounds that children love to imitate; words have meanings! They can bring harm or they can bring comfort. As expectant parents, we already have the desire to guard our children's delicate ears.

> *God, tame our tongues and make us sensitive to little ears. Help us to learn self-restraint as we communicate with our little ones.*

REFLECTING ON MY ATTITUDE TOWARD WORK

"Chore time; up and at 'em." Every Saturday morning Dad's voice would interrupt my sleep.

"Come on, sleepyhead, up and at 'em!"

I knew that there was grass to be cut or snow to be shoveled or toilet bowls to be scrubbed—hardly motivation to get up. If I got up quickly, though, Mom would make me cheese toast and let me watch cartoons for thirty minutes. After breakfast, it was time to take care of business.

Despite my complaints (both spoken and silent), I slowly learned about the many responsibilities involved in daily living. I learned to care for my own possessions as well as for my family's needs. After a while, I even learned the satisfaction of working hard to complete a task.

Obviously, we can go overboard with our work habits and become workaholics who ignore family and self. Studies have shown that fathers tend to spend more time at work after the arrival of children, perhaps because they don't want to face the increased workload at home or perhaps because the financial pressures of having children are so overwhelming. Therefore, it's important to reflect on our attitudes toward work before our lives become even more complicated by children.

God designed us to take delight in work. Work itself is not a curse; God worked to create the universe, and he gave Adam and Eve responsibilities in the Garden before the Fall. We can even reflect our faith in our attitudes when we treat the performance of our duties as a blessing rather than drudgery.

Now that it's our turn to teach work habits, we hope that our children will watch us do our work cheerfully, thankful for the chance to be useful.

God, we dedicate ourselves to instilling in our little ones a sense of the goodness of work. Remind us of how blessed we are to be able to complete the tasks that we have been given.

REFLECTING ON TRUTHFULNESS

PROVERBS
12:17–22
The LORD detests lying lips, but he delights in men who are truthful (v. 22).

Recently I was called in to serve on a jury at the county courthouse. I thought for a while about using our "situation" (the babies) as an excuse to get out of the duty, plotting elaborate exaggerations about Lisa's health and imminent trips to the doctor. As I sat there watching people give the judge such obvious half-truths about their own situations, I decided instead to fulfill my civic obligation.

During the trial, I was struck by the nervousness of the witnesses. One fellow's upraised right hand shook visibly as he took the oath to tell the truth, the whole truth, and nothing but the truth. I must admit that I trusted that fellow's testimony; he obviously took his truthfulness seriously. Somehow I felt glad that I hadn't weaseled out of my responsibility by using half-truths (well, okay, lies) about not being able to serve on the jury panel.

Nowadays many people demonstrate a very casual attitude toward the truth. Everywhere we look, we see responsible adults who lie. Lawyers quibble over subtle shadings of definition. Cheaters are celebrated for their cunning, and comedians lampoon integrity as quaint and old-fashioned. Even our consumer culture is based on surrounding ourselves with "stuff" that creates a false image about our personal wealth. Truthfulness gets lost in our anxiety over how we look and over what kinds of impressions we will make. This same fear of others rather than of God lies at the root of lying (we withhold the truth about ourselves because we fear how others may respond to it).

One of the greatest challenges we face in adulthood is the maintenance of integrity. We always have known that the world at large watches how Christians behave, but as future parents the burden of this challenge is even more immediate. Our children will listen to us speaking in the privacy of our households. As they grow older, they will observe our speedometers in a school zone. Gradually, our children will figure out just how truthful we actually are, and they will very likely set their own standard of truthfulness based at least partly on our standard. If we are going to give the gift of truthfulness to our children, we will have to be vigilant, continually reflecting on the examples we set for them.

God, help us to embrace truthfulness and honor. Remind us that you are Truth and that honesty demonstrates our respect for you.

REFLECTING ON AFFECTION

> ## COLOSSIANS
> ### 3:21
> *Fathers, do not embitter your children, or they will become discouraged.*

The prospect of fatherhood has made me reflect on the fathers whom I have known and observed. Some were gruff and abusive; others were cuddly and wise. Some were cold and reserved; others were almost embarrassing with their affection. Often I could tell when I entered the doors of a friend's house what the relationship was like between the father and his children. Some homes made me want to move right in; the love between the parents and their children was completely evident through kind words and abundant tenderness. In other households, I hated even to sit on the couch because of the tension that permeated the air. The very fibers in the furniture seemed to be seared by caustic comments and angry stares. I still remember waiting in one friend's car while he ran into the house to get his softball glove. Even from the driveway, I could hear his dad shouting orders and insults at him from the minute my buddy went in the door to the minute he came out and slammed it behind him. Back in the car, he tried to shake off his father's words, but his embarrassed and defeated demeanor told the story of his hurt.

So many of my adolescent friends wanted desperately to know that their parents loved them. Trying to fill this emptiness in their lives, they turned to destructive activities involving sex, drugs, and alcohol. If only their parents had filled these spaces early on with plenty of hugs and frequent "I love you's," perhaps their children would not have had so many difficulties in adolescence.

Our heavenly Father provided an incredible gift of unconditional love to each of us. Jesus' death and resurrection demonstrated God's tender love for humanity. We want to be parents who demonstrate love and encouragement for our household with both verbal and physical displays of affection. When our love is both unconditional and undeniable, our children will not be embittered and will learn to love others in the same way.

Father, you love us in an amazing way. Help us to demonstrate, unconditionally, your boundless love to our little ones.

IMPORTANT OTHERS

OTHERS

RUTH 4:13–17
Then Naomi took the child, laid him in her lap and cared for him
(v. 16).

Pregnancy has turned all of our relationships upside down. Lisa's little sister, who was only twelve when Lisa and I met, is now an aunt, or soon will be. The brother with whom I wrestled on our living room floor will be an uncle, and the people I've always called "Mom" and "Dad" are now "Grandma" and "Grandpa."

In fact, practically everyone we meet has taken on a new role based on the relationship they will have with our children. At church, I wonder as I shake hands with the woman in the pew behind me if she will one day be my children's Sunday school teacher. As I walk by the nursery now, I notice the smiles and tenderness on the workers' faces and not just their blue smocks. When the children's choir stands up to sing, I pay attention to the gentle enthusiasm of the director, wondering if he will be the one to train my little ones' voices to sing praises to God.

When we meet our friends' babies or hear of friends who are expecting, we realize that their little ones will be our children's playmates, future dates, and maybe even spouses! The schoolteacher I meet at the grocery store may one day teach my children. The crossing guard who signals me to stop may one day guide my children safely across the street.

In looking at people around me in this way, I have come to three conclusions. First, the realization that many people will participate in the upbringing of our children takes some of the pressure off us as parents. Not all of the lessons our children will learn will come from us.

Naomi probably didn't know the important role she played in God's plan, but the writer of the book of Ruth makes a point to tell us that her influence was important. The child for whom she cared was King David's grandfather (and therefore an ancestor of Jesus).

Lisa and I are blessed to have people in our lives who mirror traits we want our children to have. We look forward to seeing how Aunt Tina's servant heart, Grandma's creativity and strength, and Grandpa's generosity and thoughtfulness will influence our children's lives. We thank God for the many positive role models our children will have.

Second, as I look at all the people necessary to raise a child, I have a greater sense of community with my neighbors, friends, and relatives. I realize more than ever that God created us to live in relationship with each other, depending on one another. Some of these people will have a minor influence while others will impact our little ones' lives profoundly, but each will be valuable to our children and to us. Surely, Ruth was grateful that Naomi shared the responsibility for taking care of little Obed. As I notice the valuable contributions of those I meet, I live with a persistent attitude of gratefulness.

Third, I feel a desire to begin praying now for the people who will take care of our little ones, from the neonatal nurses to their grandmas and grandpas. Some of these people will be skilled at taking care of children; some will be rusty; some will just be learning. All will need prayer. We pray that God will use them to bless our children with tender care and that, in turn, our babies will be blessings to them.

God, thank you for all the "others" who will be involved in our children's lives. Make them strong examples of Christlikeness. Teach us always to be thankful for their care.

GODLY GRANDPARENTS

**2 TIMOTHY
1:1–7**

*I have been reminded
of your sincere faith,
which first lived in
your grandmother
Lois and in your
mother Eunice and, I
am persuaded, now
lives in you also
(v. 5).*

Although I lived more than a thousand miles from my grandparents when I was a child, my parents made this relationship a priority. Every vacation, usually twice a year, we traveled from New York or Virginia to visit and to honor my parents' parents, all of whom lived in Mississippi. In the last years of Grandfather Fant's life, I was privileged to live close enough to visit more frequently. As I spent more time with Grandfather, I was amazed to recognize in him some of our shared physical features, gestures, traits, and inclinations, from our large hat size to our love of books. Even though our contact had been limited to two visits a year for most of my young life, his impact on me is evident.

At church last Sunday, I introduced myself to a man sitting nearby.

"Are you Tommy's grandson?" the white-haired man inquired with a mixture of surprise and delight as he shook my hand. He continued to grip my palm while he searched my face for my grandfather's likeness.

"Yes, sir, I am," I said proudly.

"He came to our church forty-some years ago to preach a revival. He was a great preacher," replied the gentleman.

Since I moved to Mississippi as an adult, I have grown accustomed to people asking me whether I am related to Tommy (Thomas Edison Fant). After twenty years as a plant supervisor for Masonite, twenty years as a pastor, and thirty years in the dog kennel business, Grandfather Fant knew everyone. How grateful I am to be the grandson of someone people remember as a man of God. How grateful I am to have had parents who saw the significance of the grandparent-child relationship!

Lisa's pregnancy has started me thinking about our parents' involvement in our children's lives. Grandparents influence their grandchildren's lives in ways that parents cannot. Our children will be blessed to have heaps of loving acceptance and attention from all of their grandparents, but I'm particularly thankful that my children will have a legacy of faith from my parents and from my in-laws. Just as Lisa's grandmother led her to Christ, her own parents will likewise have a godly influence on our children's lives. Lisa's folks are already wearing out their pants' knees praying for them. As for my parents, our children will have the opportunity, as I did, to answer with pride and gratefulness that Gene, Sr., and Mona—who have ministered through preaching and music all over the world—are their grandparents.

Timothy had a holy grandmother, an early convert who established faith as a family experience. Her influence on the young Timothy helped to change the course of history. If your parents are Christians, you can thank God for the legacy of faith they will pass on to your children. If they are not Christians, you can still follow God's commandment to honor them by respecting their rights to have a relationship with your children.

Father, make our children's grandparents into bold examples of faith. May Christlikeness be our family heritage.

SIBLINGS

My brother, Steve, is two years younger than I, an age difference that practically guarantees bitter rivalry. We shared a bed until I was in the fifth grade because we lived in a parsonage that had no extra bedrooms. During the day, we fought constantly, disputing over which television show to watch, what the rules of a game were, and who would ride in the front seat of the car. Our verbal disputes quickly escalated into shouting matches, then insult competitions, and finally physical confrontations where fists, toys, and even furniture would fly, sending our mother nearly to her wits' end.

Even at that stage of our lives, however, we showed glimmers of putting aside our rivalries as, every night at bedtime, we became fast friends. As partners in crime, we created every imaginable excuse and silliness to stay up past our bedtime. We tickled, giggled, told jokes, became puppeteers for our stuffed animals, and generally pushed the limit of our dad's patience.

Our parents were elated when we moved to a larger house where they could finally separate us. Surely they must have prayed fervently and wearily for wisdom in how to best teach us to love one another so that we wouldn't kill each other.

Despite all our fraternal feuding, we (and our parents) survived and grew out of the rivalry. We each served as best man at the other's wedding. We have stayed close, though Steve now lives about 1,200 miles away in New Mexico. Indeed, my most treasured memory of growing up with Steve is that of our public professions of faith during the same service on Good Friday, 1971. Even our spiritual lives have been intertwined closely.

Have you ever noticed how many siblings were involved with Christ's inner circle? Andrew and Simon; James and John; Mary, Martha, and Lazarus; Jesus' own brother James. Can you imagine being Simon Peter's brother? Those Zebedee boys (literally, "sons of thunder") probably fought like crazy when they were younger. That family dwelling must have grown small very quickly for their parents. Sibling rivalries are nothing new to our age! Certainly as these brothers and sisters grew into young men and women and began to follow Christ as disciples, their sibling status must have helped them in their ministries.

Many expectant parents already have children who may have mixed emotions about a new brother or sister. For these parents, an important task of pregnancy is to prepare the older child (or children) for the new arrival. After all, the newborn will forever alter the dynamics of the family's life. Taking time to engage the older child in the joys of pregnancy and the excitement of the birth of a new sibling will help him or her welcome the new arrival. Likewise, meeting the child's need for security and extra attention now can pay off later when the new baby demands that parents divide their time. Finally, instilling early on the sense that the older child is his "brother's keeper"—that being an older sibling comes with the responsibility of caring for younger sisters and brothers, a responsibility that is worthwhile. (If Cain had felt responsible for Abel's well-being, their lives would not have ended so tragically.) Even with the best of preparations, the jealousies that can arise between siblings may be dismaying, but we can take hope in these New Testament biblical examples that with God's help our children will find not only friends but spiritual allies in their siblings.

God, help us prepare our children for the arrival of this new life. Make us sensitive to all of our children's needs. Give us wisdom as we encourage our children to love and appreciate each other.

DOCTORS

LUKE 5:17–32
*Jesus answered them,
"It is not the healthy
who need a doctor,
but the sick. I have
not come to call the
righteous, but sinners
to repentance"*
(vv. 31–32).

Our relationship with doctors began long before I became pregnant. For three years, the specialists at the University Medical Center searched for reasons behind and remedies for our infertility. We were regular patients for so long, I felt strangely sad when I realized that, now that I was pregnant, I would no longer be under their care. At eight weeks of pregnancy, when they felt confident all was going well, we said good-bye. We would have to find another doctor to bring these babies into the world.

Notwithstanding the jokes about women's crushes on their male obstetricians, couples really do feel a special bond with the man or woman who brings their little miracle into the world. Many a baby (Gene's dad, among them) has been named after the doctor who performed the delivery. Near the end of pregnancy, your physician is like an old friend who checks up on you every week.

When we chose our obstetrician, we talked to many friends and sought their advice. We had all the practical considerations like insurance, location, billing policies, and so forth, but we also knew we needed someone to whom we felt comfortable entrusting not only my health but also our babies' health. We hoped we could find someone who didn't let the frequency of seeing babies come into the world dampen his or her wonder at the miracle. We wanted someone who would understand that although we might be only one couple among maybe hundreds of patients, to us our babies are the most important, beautiful, and special in the world. This doctor would share unparalleled intimacy with us and would be the first person our children would meet as they entered the world.

After several weeks of consideration and prayer, we interviewed one doctor and decided right on the spot that he was our choice. My obstetrician is a wonderful godly man with an easy bedside manner who has helped to make the pregnancy much less anxious. We even found that we are members of the same church. On Sunday mornings, I sometimes point out where he and his family are seated (you know, just in case).

Selecting a pediatrician has been another important decision. This doctor will take care of our little ones as they grow. Memories of this person will linger with our children for the rest of their lives, establishing first attitudes toward medicine and health. After perhaps even more investigation than we had done for the obstetrician, we finally settled on a local doctor with whom we feel both we and our children will be comfortable. Children love his colorful ties and quick humor; parents appreciate his skill and self-assured demeanor.

We forget sometimes that our doctors can actually help us to understand the work of Christ, the Great Physician. When Luke, a doctor himself, writes of Christ's healing the paralyzed man, he draws obvious parallels between physical healing and spiritual wholeness. Our physicians encourage us to live healthy lifestyles, diagnose and heal our complications, help us manage pain, calm our fears, and ultimately help us to produce healthy babies. As the Great Physician, Christ teaches us to live abundantly, he diagnoses and heals us of our sin sickness, teaches us to persevere through painful times, replaces our fears with peace, and empowers us to produce fruit.

What a blessing good doctors and nurses are! Their healing touch eases many an anxious moment. We don't fully understand the title Great Physician unless we have had a good physician in our own lives. Our doctors actually help us to understand more about God!

God, lead us to skillful doctors and nurses who will be used by you to bring health to our physical bodies. Help us to understand more about you and your powerful role as the healer of our souls.

MENTORS

> TITUS 2:1–14
> *Then they can train
> the younger women to
> love their husbands
> and children (v. 4).*

Waiting until later in life to have children definitely has advantages. I was the oldest child in my family, always the trailblazer, always the first in my generation to reach important milestones—the first to go to kindergarten, the first to date, the first to go to college, the first to marry. In having children, however, I'm nowhere near the first. For this milestone, I have plenty of family members and friends who know the perils and the perks of pregnancy and from whose experience I can benefit. Even Gene's sister-in-law, Kathy, who is pregnant now, is due about four months before I am.

Although many of these women are younger than I, their prior experiences of pregnancy have made them valuable mentors to me. "When did you stop feeling morning sickness?" I asked Kathy, hoping her answer would be whatever week of pregnancy I was in at the time. "When did you start wearing maternity clothes?" I questioned Amy, who said she'd send me hers. "What kind of stroller did you buy for your twins?" I inquired of Anna, who offered to go shopping with me. My lists of questions have been endless, yet these "experts" have answered tirelessly.

Not only did they give advice, these women also shared encouraging words: "We are so excited for you guys!" "We know you're going to make great parents." "Two babies will be really hard at first, so I want to come and help!" "You cannot imagine how much you will love them" came the heartening words of wisdom from these mentoring mothers.

Although they don't often admit it, men also need mentoring networks. One of Gene's first activities after he found out we were having twins was to hop on the Internet to find out what other fathers of twins were saying about the experience of parenting multiples. Since then, he has established camaraderie with some Christian friends and relatives with whom he can talk when he has those burning questions that bother first-time dads: "When did you get to start sleeping again?" "What did you do in the delivery room?" and "Will I be able to play golf again?"

Having others to whom we could turn for advice and encouragement has been a real blessing, and Paul notes in his letter to Titus that such behavior is to be sanctioned in the fellowship of believers. The older (or more experienced, in our case) can train the younger to apply Christian principles to daily living, to live faithfully in their family relationships so that they, in turn, can be examples of Christian living.

Probably many people mentor others without thinking about the spiritual implications. Most of us love to feel that we are knowledgeable and that our advice is valued. However, the natural act of mentoring can be a real ministry if it is directed by the Holy Spirit. Although the women who have helped me may not have consciously seen their advice as "spiritual," the Bible certainly shows the value of practical wisdom. (The entire book of Proverbs is devoted to practical advice to the young.) Teaching, helping, and encouraging others are always activities of spiritual import.

As Christians, we talk about our responsibility to be good stewards of our money, our possessions, our talents, and even our time, but rarely do we see the knowledge and wisdom given to us through life's experiences as a commodity that we are responsible for sharing. The experiences that we are having now will prepare us to help others, just as others are helping us.

God, bless those who have blessed us with practical wisdom and encouragement. Remind us of our responsibility as workers in your kingdom to mentor others.

PETS

We acquired our cat, Jeepers, when we didn't think we would ever have children of our own. We guess that lots of young couples get dogs and cats to take the place of babies, even if for only a while. We hope that Jeepers will be around for a long time because pets can add such joy to our lives. We have fun imagining our little girl dressing up our cat or our little boy chasing it through the house. We know that taking care of a pet can also teach our children about many life experiences: companionship, responsibility, and death.

Jeepers has adjusted well to my pregnancy. She enjoys the extra naps I take because she gets to join me, curled up on my warm tummy. There our three "babies" sleep peacefully, two sucking their thumbs and one purring. (In one of those wild pregnancy nightmares, I actually dreamed once I gave birth to three kittens!) We joke that after the babies are born, we will have to put Jeepers in the crib with them to put them to sleep. (Of course, we are actually more worried about how to keep the cat *out* of the cribs!) Of all those neat little gadgets that supposedly simulate womb sounds to calm a fussy infant, I've never heard one include the sound of purring.

When we found out that we were expecting, Gene looked at Jeepers and said, "You aren't our baby anymore. You just became a cat!" Truthfully, we are a little concerned about how Jeepers will fit in to our new family situation. Her manners are horrible. She must have had a vampire for a father because she greets anyone who offers affection by clamping her little cat fangs on any exposed body parts (wrists, ankles, neck, etc.). We have tried to break her of this habit but, being a cat, she resists all efforts at training. Indeed, dealing with a jealous pet may be another one of the adjustments we have to make when the babies come.

While the Bible doesn't have much to say about pets, there is a special relationship described between Adam and the creatures of Eden. In fact, God used the animals to provide Adam with his first object lesson: animals are wonderful, but people are even better company. As God paraded the animals in front of Adam, it became painfully clear that none of them could be a "suitable helper" for Adam. Adam needed a human being to find true companionship; he needed a partner, and none of the animals were up to that level. Thus God made Eve, the perfect flesh-and-bone partner.

As much as we love our pets, we have to keep in mind that people are our first priority. When pets interfere with our relationship with our spouse or endanger our children, they have to take second place. This is a really touchy issue for a lot of expectant couples because usually one partner has more of an attachment to the pet than the other. Having children will mean making some adjustments that protect both the child and the pet. Sometimes this will mean that the pet's freedoms may be restricted; sometimes this will mean giving up the pet to someone whose home life is better suited to meeting the pet's needs.

Although we may not know how Jeepers will fit in when the babies come, we do know that we will be able to work out an arrangement that strengthens our unity as marriage partners, protects our children, and shows respect for the creatures of God's world.

Creator, thank you for the companionship pets provide us. Teach us to care for them as you entrusted us to do in Eden. Remind us that people come first.

GRANDCHILDREN

PSALM 78:1–8

He decreed statutes for Jacob and established the law in Israel, which he commanded our forefathers to teach their children, so the next generation would know them, even the children yet to be born, and they in turn would tell their children (vv. 5–6).

When I was a child, I always looked forward to attending my maternal grandfather's family reunion, the Lowe family July Fourth celebration, where I would see my two great-grandparents and the families of their nine children. Although shy, I loved to be acknowledged by each of those great-aunts and great-uncles because I admired them and felt so proud to be among their kin. I loved to hear stories of how this large family had made it through the Great Depression without much in the way of material goods, but with obvious happiness because of their faith. While the homemade ice cream was definitely my favorite part of the reunion, the singing ranked a close second. When the Lowe family sang—with Aunt Ina Raye hitting the high notes—I felt that the heavenly choirs surely were listening to the testimonies of God's love and work in this family's life. On an upcoming July Fourth, the Lowes will have their fiftieth reunion. What a legacy!

It is said that the best way to fight our own mortality is to have children. They are the only guarantee that we will leave some lasting contribution in this world. Did you know that before they are even born, baby girls' ovaries contain all of the eggs they will ever have? Just think about it: the seeds that may become our grandchildren are already in my womb! Three generations are represented in our one pregnancy.

As we think about our descendants, we already feel a responsibility to our children and to our children's children. Future generations will reap either the consequences of our sins or the benefits of our godliness. Generations of Israelites lost out on God's blessings because their forefathers neglected to keep the faith. Nevertheless, God has always had a faithful remnant who taught their children well.

In teaching our children about God's righteousness, we will be laying the path for our children to do the same, and for their children, as well. We will be playing a part in the training of future generations of believers who will worship God. We hope someday to be the grandparents of little girls and boys who will receive a spiritual inheritance from us.

God, you have placed us in a chain of generations that have faithfully worshiped you. Remind us of our responsibilities as we continue the work of those who have given us a foundation.

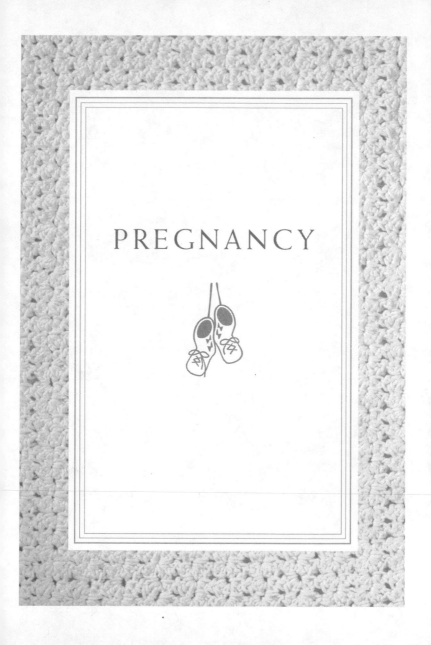

PREGNANCY

A TIME TO BE PREGNANT

I've been inspired by pregnancy to write my own version of Ecclesiastes 3:

There is a time for pregnancy, and a season for every ailment under heaven.
There is a time for heartburn and a time for cravings,
A time for feeling tired and a time for feeling energized,
A time for sex and a time for abstaining,
A time for the pains of childbirth and a time for the joys of childbirth.

While my version may not be as poignant as the biblical one or as melodic as the Byrds' musical rendition of the '60s, it does remind me to put the experience of pregnancy into proper perspective. Pregnancy is a temporary condition; it will be over before we know it. In the larger scheme of life, these brief periods of discomfort and inconvenience are hardly remembered and, in a strange way, may be missed when they are over.

The advice most often given to us throughout our pregnancy has been to remember that all stages of parenthood, from conception to graduation, are temporary—they only last for a season. Reminding ourselves of the brevity of each situation can help us savor the seasons of life. We can embrace heartburn and fatigue (and the wife who is experiencing them) as the stuff life is made of, as the conditions that are part of the miraculous experience of pregnancy, and as normal, healthy indicators of the life growing within. Our attitude determines whether there is joy in the journey as well as in reaching the goal.

Lord, teach us to find contentment in every circumstance through Jesus Christ who gives us strength. Help us to enjoy the rhythm of our life's experiences.

BUT LORD, I CAN'T SEE —— MY FEET!

> ## PROVERBS 31:30
> *Charm is deceptive,*
> *and beauty is fleeting;*
> *but a woman who*
> *fears the LORD is to*
> *be praised.*

I remember the first time I went shopping for maternity clothes. Since I was just starting to show, I felt a little awkward as I looked at those pants with the unattractive stretchy front panel inserts. A woman who was obviously more at ease amidst the racks of tent dresses than I struck up a conversation. "How many are you having?" she asked.

"Excuse me?" I responded.

"How many babies are you having? This is my third pregnancy, and I'm having twins this time," she bragged in a loud voice.

"Oh, me too," I said distractedly as I was trying to figure out how sizes in maternity clothes were determined and what size dress I would wear three months from now.

The woman looked a little disappointed that she hadn't cornered the market on twin pregnancies, but she continued in her loud, confident voice, describing how large I would get with twins. She mentioned weight gains that would have doubled my size and quoted bra sizes that I didn't know existed. At that point I was feeling embarrassed by her candor and overwhelmed by what I imagined myself to look like at the end of nine months. I tried inching away from her to look at another rack of clothing, but she didn't take the hint.

I quickly determined I wasn't quite ready for the world of maternity fashions and left the store without a purchase, bewildered and dismayed.

Now I'm quite comfortable in my maternity clothes. The weight gain has been gradual, so I've had time to get used to the new body. However, I have to admit that occasionally I fight the desire to cringe when I step on the scales, and I can't help but be a little dismayed that my feet are disappearing beneath the awning of my protruding tummy. I know that the weight gain is necessary to the health of our babies, but my cultural mind-set wars with my common sense. In a culture that exalts superthin models and spends millions on cosmetic surgery, coping with a growing waistline, stretch marks, swollen ankles, and skin blemishes, even in pregnancy, can be difficult.

Indeed, both husbands and wives may be concerned about the pregnant silhouette, worrying that the familiar prepregnant body will never return. We have to remind ourselves that these changes are temporary. Eventually, the waistline will shrink to an approximation of its former size, and most of the stretch marks and blemishes will fade. Although the once-familiar body may not return exactly as it was, we both will enjoy getting to know the new one! Additionally, we can appreciate the magnificence of God's design. Husbands, who are more objective than their pregnant wives, can help them see the attractiveness of their pregnant form.

Furthermore, pregnancy is a good time to evaluate our attitudes toward the ideal of womanly beauty, leaving our adolescent obsession with a cover-girl look to focus on improving the beauty of our characters. The writer of Proverbs warns us that a charming and beautiful woman is here today and gone tomorrow. (Just look at magazine covers of the last twenty years. Not many beautiful faces and slim figures stick around that long.) Yet a woman who respects God will be honored for eternity. In the long run, your husband and your children will admire you for the beauty of your character, not for your figure.

Lord, teach us to cultivate right attitudes about outer and inner beauty that we can pass on to our children. Focus our attention on the eternal beauty that derives from your wisdom.

> **EPHESIANS**
> **5:15–16**
> *Be very careful, then,
> how you live—not
> as unwise but as wise,
> making the most of
> every opportunity,
> because the days
> are evil.*

My mom used to make a difficult commute to work each day. Not only did she have to travel a long distance, but she also encountered heavy traffic, poor roads, and a drawbridge that opened regularly for shipping traffic. Rather than sit and fume in the stop-and-go traffic or let her blood pressure rise when her car was at a standstill for an hour or more, she learned to make lemonade out of lemons. She always had some project in the car to work on during these delays. It was amazing what she could get done by whittling away at a project during several consecutive days of those dead-in-your-tracks traffic jams. Sometimes she would balance her checkbook or write letters; sometimes she clipped coupons or even did needlework. Once she crocheted an entire afghan!

I know several women who have been put on extensive bed rest during their pregnancies. (I'm thankful that I have not been.) One, Alice, was on bed rest for six weeks before her daughter Christina was born. Although following her doctor's strict instructions to limit movement from the bed to the bathroom to the couch was difficult, she looks back at this time now as one of the most precious periods in her family life. "Being confined to the bed gave me a lot of quality time with Cassie, who was four at the time," she said. "She would crawl up on the bed with me, and we would play board games, read books, do craft projects, take naps, and snuggle. She became my best helper and my playmate. If I hadn't been forced to be still, I would have spent some of that precious time on my long list of to-do's instead of on my relationship with Cassie."

With so many tasks to finalize and so many distractions in our lives, it's easy to let our time dribble-drabble away, leaving us with frustrations and interrupted priorities. My mother learned very quickly that she could utilize her time in the car or waste it in aggravation. Alice learned to use her prescribed bed rest as a gift, an opportunity to spend unparalleled quality time with her daughter.

We can take advantage of every opportunity to use our moments for God's glory, or we can miss the opportunities he gives us.

Lord, teach us to make the most of our opportunities. Help us to remember that our time is valuable and that even the delays that we may face are gifts to use for your glory.

BOY OR GIRL?

> ## GENESIS 1:27
> *So God created man in his own image, in the image of God he created him; male and female he created them.*

Alex and Nina had chosen not to find out the sex of their baby before birth. They relished the idea of a surprise. They got one. Future grandparents, aunts, uncles, and friends who knew the estimated size of the baby to be large had nearly all guessed that Nina was having a boy. Even strangers, depending on the wisdom of old wives' tales, had said that Nina's glowing, healthy complexion was a sure sign that she was carrying a boy. Although they didn't let on, Alex and Nina secretly expected that all that vigorous kicking surely had to come from a bouncing baby boy. When the obstetrician delivered the baby and said, "It's a girl!" Nina's first response was, "A girl? Are you sure?" The doctor replied, "Yes, I've delivered quite a few babies, and I can guarantee that this one is a girl." Nina was not only surprised, she was elated. For her, the joy of the experience of birth was multiplied because of this delightful surprise.

We, on the other hand, wanted to know the sexes of our babies as soon as possible. Because we were having twins, we wanted as much information as possible to prepare for the arrival of two little bundles of joy. Being a multiple pregnancy, which is always considered high risk, I had already experienced several sonograms, each one providing us with a beautiful picture of our little ones' growth *in utero*. But like many couples, we especially looked forward to the sonogram that would reveal the sex of our babies.

On the big day, the sonogram technician showed us into the spacious room in the back of the office suite. She helped me get up onto the examining table and jellied my pregnant tummy. The monitor was positioned so that we could watch the results together. Our eyes adjusted to the shapes and shadows that, without the guidance of our technician, would have seemed meaningless. We marveled at how our little ones had developed. Their legs, arms, hearts, and ribs were all visible in the secret world of amniotic fluid.

Soon the technician zeroed in on "Baby A" in just the right position to give a full view of his maleness. "It's a boy," she said matter-of-factly. Neither of us doubted her; we definitely could see a boy. We must have been a little dumbstruck because the technician looked up as if waiting for a response. Somehow knowing the sex of our baby all of a sudden made him (him!) more real to us. I was thrilled but also a little nervous. I didn't have brothers and had never been around little boys very much. We had hoped for one boy, but how would I handle twin boys? We waited silently for the technician to identify the sex of the other baby.

"Baby B is definitely a girl," she stated.

"Are you sure?" I asked apprehensively. I had heard of couples thinking they had a girl from the sonogram and then getting a big surprise when the baby was born.

"Are you sure it's a girl?" I asked again.

"Yep, I'm positive. She's in a perfect position to make the determination. This is a textbook picture of a girl."

What joy we had that day as we left the doctor's office! A boy and a girl. A matched set.

Probably the first question people ask when they find out that you're expecting is, "Boy or girl?" We love to see the looks on their faces when we answer, "Both!" No matter how much we might try to break the stereotypes of pink and blue by decorating our nursery in primary colors or by encouraging our girls to play sports and our boys to appreciate the arts, we know that there are differences between male and female that go beyond our cultural stereotypes and anatomical differences. Best-selling books have made a fortune playing up these stereotypes in their advice offerings. We know that men and women are different and, despite our bewilderment and exasperation sometimes at the problems that such differences cause, we also know that these differences add variety, joy, and a little mystery to our lives. We care about maleness and femaleness because these are God-designed distinctions. God is so wise in creating us as males and females. He made the world an infinitely more interesting place with that one simple division.

God, thank you for making us the way we are, male and female. Thank you for the joy that little girls and little boys bring us. Guide us as we teach our children to appreciate and respect differences between the sexes.

> ROMANS 7:14–
> 8:2
> *I do not understand
> what I do. For what I
> want to do I do not
> do, but what I hate I
> do (v. 15).*

Jana felt out of control in her first trimester. The slightest irritation would infuriate her. Mike, not realizing at first that her behavior was triggered by the chemical warfare raging in her body, was quick to retaliate, further fueling Jana's exasperation. Before long, her anger would escalate into a rage that was completely out of character. At one point, Jana was so out of control, she began to hyperventilate.

After speaking to her doctor, Jana and Mike realized that her behavior was related to her pregnancy and probably temporary. To avert future outbursts, however, any time Mike perceived that Jana was about to lose her composure, he would curb his own desire to respond antagonistically and quietly leave the room to give her time to regain self-control. When he would return a few minutes later to check on her, the fury had usually passed. By the second trimester, those same hormones that had wreaked such havoc were giving Jana renewed energy and an overwhelming sense of well-being.

Although Jana's case is extreme, many women feel out of control at some point during pregnancy because of the hormonal turbulence raging in their bodies. This situation is frustrating for both husbands and wives. Expectant dads are confused that rational discourse just doesn't work, while moms feel like helpless passengers on an emotional roller coaster. As much as we are fascinated by the miracle of the human form in pregnancy, we are also reminded of the limitations of our bodies. As pregnant women, we may feel like slaves to our physical bodies, controlled by hormones, discomfort, and sleep deprivation. As expectant fathers, our sinful natures wage war against our desire to be understanding, patient, and self-controlled with our spouses.

Jesus sympathizes with our condition, for he has known the restrictions of being human. He knows what it is to be physically taxed—hungry, thirsty, tired, hot, in pain—yet, he never gave in to the temptation to allow those physical concerns to dictate his attitudes or actions. He knows what it is to deal with people who are emotionally unstable, angry, difficult, and out of sorts; still, he was always self-controlled, always in perfect harmony with the Father, always acting out of love. Through his life and death, Jesus won the victory over our human frailty. In him we are not slaves to our fleshly weaknesses, but free to live according to the Spirit.

Pray about whatever ailments concern you, particularly those that are affecting your walk in the Spirit. God can give you both practical wisdom and power to live triumphantly despite your physical encumbrances.

Lord, give us unusual patience with others and with ourselves in these days. Make us longsuffering in our love and encouraging in our words.

THE COMPARISON WAY OF LIFE

EXODUS 20:17
You shall not covet your neighbor's house. You shall not covet your neighbor's wife, or his manservant or maidservant, his ox or donkey, or anything that belongs to your neighbor.

We used to get frustrated that everyone our age already had children and that we had not yet been able to have a baby. One time we saw a couple with beautiful twins, and Gene whispered to me (not entirely tongue-in-cheek), "Look at those people! They are hogging all the babies! It's not fair!" Of course, now that we are expecting twins, I am humbled by the irony of his previous comments.

An amazing phenomenon about this comparison way of life is that we look only at the surface in our coveting. Our vision loses clear focus: we see only the good in others, never the bad; and we see only the bad in our own lives, and never the good. We desire only the "positive" things (cars, clothes, houses, slim figures, children), and we look past, or are ignorant of, the negative (debt, physical or emotional illness, and secret marital strife).

The subtle lifestyle of comparison really quenches our joys. At one time we were guilty of coveting our neighbor's children; we had defined our lives by what we lacked rather than by what we had: heaps of God-given blessings. In the process we had sapped ourselves of valuable mental and spiritual energy by constantly looking in the wrong direction for happiness and self-worth.

Although we may not have someone else's amazingly smooth pregnancy or elegantly petite pregnant figure, we can rejoice in the goodness of God's blessings. When we focus our comparison on God's incredible love for us, we will find ourselves refreshed.

Lord, give us perspective to view your blessings. Keep us both humble and grateful in all aspects of our lives.

KEEPING A SENSE OF HUMOR

Since I am eight months pregnant with twins, I'm very round at this point. Picking something up off of the floor is a real challenge, and most of the time I have to ask Gene to tie my shoes because I cannot reach over my pregnant belly.

I was at the post office the other day, my arms full of packages. The line was a mile long, and my back was killing me. As I waited for my turn, I kept dropping packages. Each time I clumsily bent over to pick them up, I felt the eyes of those around me watching attentively, but no one offered to help. I figured that people thought I looked big enough to go into labor at any moment and were worried they might have to assist in the birth. Before I reached the counter, I must have dropped packages four or five times, and, of course, I had to navigate picking them up. By the time I left the post office, I was totally flustered.

As I related this story to Gene and my sister, Tina, that evening, I kept imagining what those folks must have thought each time I dropped something: "Look at that huge pregnant woman bending over to pick up her packages." While I was frustrated with my huge size and my inability to complete tasks I once did with ease, I decided that no one wanted to help me because they were too amused watching me try to pick up the packages myself. We all began to laugh at what a scene I had made and, instead of feeling angry and embarrassed, I began to laugh about my predicament.

Keeping a sense of humor makes life so much more pleasant than when you take everything seriously. One of the golden nuggets of wisdom we've been given by friends who are parents is to keep a sense of humor. When babies are screaming at 2 A.M., when you're frustrated at learning to breast-feed, when you are confronted with the smelliest dirty diapers or sour baby spit-up on the shirt you just changed, keep your sense of humor. It will do your heart good.

God, renew us with the good medicine of laughter. Remind us to be careful about taking ourselves too seriously.

ANXIETIES

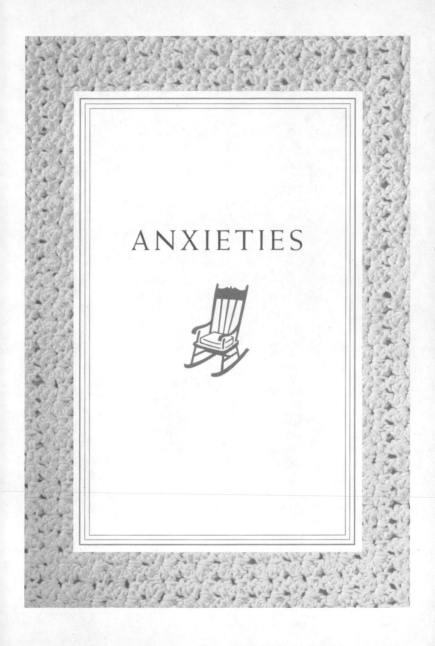

DON'T BE AFRAID!

MARK 6:45–56
*"Take courage! It is I.
Don't be afraid"*
(v. 50).

I have never been a fearful person. As a child, I was forever leading my friends on expeditions into the woods in pursuit of some imaginary foe. We would jump off rooftops and tree limbs, pretending to leap from cliffs or fast-moving trains. My mom still covers her ears when I tell stories about these adventures, saying she's surprised that I survived to adulthood; she doesn't want to know everything I endured. While I've become more cautious as an adult, I could hardly be called fearful.

Until now.

I find myself lying awake at night, worrying about those precious babies in that womb, the balance in the checking account, anything. Impending parenthood has made me overly sensitive and anxious. One night I looked in on the cat at least six times; I just wanted to make certain that she was sleeping peacefully! Each time we go to the doctor, I worry about what kind of news we will get; I almost dread the visits as much as I look forward to them. What will I do when the babies arrive and the reality of being responsible for the well-being of helpless newborns begins to sink in?

One of Christ's most common sayings to his disciples was "Don't be afraid!" Even those who walked closest to him had constant battles with fear and anxiety. This life is filled with enough worries without our adding unnecessary ones over which we have no real control. As Christians, however, we can rest in the knowledge that God is in control and cares for us.

God, help us to stop being fearful. Fill us with the confident knowledge of your providence and love.

"AS LONG AS THE BABY IS HEALTHY . . ."

> **JOHN 9:1–3**
> *"Neither this man nor his parents sinned,"* said Jesus, *"but this happened so that the work of God might be displayed in his life"* (v. 3).

Perhaps all expectant parents have found themselves using the phrase "as long as the baby is healthy." Anxiety about the health of unborn children is both universal and natural. After reading so many books about the medical aspects of pregnancy, our logic sometimes becomes overwhelmed by the ominous possibilities of what complications, maladies, and birth defects could happen to our little ones.

Though medical science has given us a better understanding of genetics and other factors affecting the growth and development of children, we can subtly and perhaps subconsciously slip into thinking like the folks during the time of Christ, attributing children's spiritual, emotional, or physical problems to the past sins of their parents. Do we secretly think that if the little ones aren't healthy we are to blame? This tendency to worry that God will "punish" us through our children reveals our lack of trust in a loving God. Jesus himself rebuffed this distorted attitude.

Certainly we must bear the responsibility and suffer the consequences of irresponsible actions. For example, mothers who drink alcohol during pregnancy may produce a baby with fetal alcohol syndrome; fathers who smoke expose their wives and unborn children to harmful chemicals. However, we find freedom in the knowledge that our simple failures will not be visited with some sort of divine retribution on our children. Just because we are sinful creatures who wrestle with our mortal nature does not mean that God will "get even" with us. Likewise, doing everything "right" doesn't guarantee that our children will be healthy. Even if our little ones are born with some sort of problems, we know that God's glory can be found in their lives and in ours.

God, help us not to be governed by the superstitious thinking that our secret sins will be found out in our children. Teach us to trust your unconditional love for us and for our children.

COURAGE

When we lived in New Orleans, we learned pretty quickly which areas to avoid, especially at night. Occasionally a friend of ours, a native of the city, would escort us to a hidden restaurant or an interesting courtyard in an area that we would have never ventured into by ourselves. Her confidence was contagious, and we soon learned how to be more adventurous without being foolish. Without that confidence that she shared with us, we would have missed out on many wonderful experiences. Our fear and anxiety would have limited us.

When I was a teenager with a new driver's license, we lived out in the country a good forty-five-minute drive from restaurants, movie theaters, the beach of that mecca of teen culture, the mall. My parents could have been overprotective of their teenage daughter, forbidding me to drive until I was more experienced, but such restrictions would have only served to increase my insecurities and fears about driving. Instead, my stepdad, with the kind of trust that inspires responsible behavior, encouraged me to venture out.

"You won't learn if you don't take the risk," he said. "Just get out there and do it!"

So, praying all the while (with my parents praying, too!), I drove out into the big world, boldly embracing the risk, my confidence increasing with each mile.

Bringing new life into the world requires courage. We are opening ourselves up to a whole new realm of vulnerabilities. We will love these little human beings more than anyone we have ever loved. Will they love us? Cause us pain? Reject us? Will we be successful parents or will we fail? Fear finds ample room to grow in our hearts as the pregnancy progresses.

Paul knew that our God is not one of timidity, but of boldness and courage. When we realize that God will help us embrace the risks of loving others boldly, we can be courageous. He will comfort us when we are afraid, and he will encourage us when we are at our most vulnerable.

Father, give us the courage to live boldly. Replace our fears with the confidence of your love.

> ### LUKE 12:25–26
> *Who of you by worrying can add a single hour to his life? Since you cannot do this very little thing, why do you worry about the rest?*
>
> ### 1 THESSALONIANS 5:16–18
> *Be joyful always; pray continually; give thanks in all circumstances, for this is God's will for you in Christ Jesus.*

We never really knew what anxiety was until these little ones came along. Gene never worried about whether car seats would fit in our vehicles. I never worried about how fast I could get the screens off the windows in the nursery (in case of fire). We never worried about the carbon monoxide levels in the back of the house or the "itchiness" of the carpets. I had never priced diaper ointment nor thought about the cost, care, and possible side effects of circumcising a little boy. Should we paint the nursery with murals? Will the colors be overstimulating? How are the child-care workers at church chosen? Much of the stress of pregnancy is caused by all of these new decisions we have to make about situations we know little or nothing about.

Jesus points out the foolishness of constant worrying. Worry diminishes our joy and our thankfulness over our blessings. Perhaps we have a new understanding of Paul's exhortation to the Thessalonians: "Pray continually!" As we pray and turn those concerns over to the God of the universe, we are released from the anxieties that plague us! Before we became expectant parents, we never had quite as much over which we worried; now we always find ourselves in prayer.

Certainly we have plenty to do in preparation for the birth of our twins, but we cannot allow the details of life to rob us of the peace and joy of this special time. We need to take care of what we can control: our overattention to worries. By praying often and praying earnestly we can be released from a part of the burdens that weigh us down.

God, this anxiety that we feel distracts us from focusing on you. Help us to keep a proper perspective, even when we feel overwhelmed. Remind us that prayer has the power to relieve us from our anxieties by drawing us closer to you and to each other.

"WHEN I HAD MY BABY . . ."

Something about a pregnant woman seems to invite other women to volunteer their best (or worst) childbirth stories. The last thing a mother-to-be (especially a first-time mother) wants to hear is graphic details of twenty-four-hour labors, ten-pound babies, and epidurals that didn't work. As a pregnant mother of twins, Lisa is constantly bombarded with tales of mothers put on bed rest and premature deliveries.

Although some of these stories are informative and useful reminders of the necessity to take care of one's self during pregnancy, occasionally people cross the line by capitalizing on the sensational rather than the inspirational. It's as if some of these people are trying to belittle our experience with their harrowing, death-defying stories.

One characteristic of a wise person is knowing when to tune out foolish, discouraging chatter. Obviously, birthing a baby has been successfully completed by at least a few billion women, and you will more than likely follow in their footsteps. Certainly, worrying will not change things and more than likely will make any possible complications worse.

Therefore, we should concentrate on the well-chosen advice of friends who seek to encourage us, remembering that it will soon be our responsibility to encourage others.

Lord, help us to recognize wise advice when we hear it, to tune out unproductive and discouraging talk, and, in the future, to think twice before sharing "our story."

DON'T DROWN IN DETAILS

PHILIPPIANS
4:6–7

Do not be anxious about anything, but in everything, by prayer and petition, with thanksgiving, present your requests to God. And the peace of God, which transcends all understanding, will guard your hearts and your minds in Christ Jesus.

I have taken up the habit of peeking into the babies' room several times a day. This act both warms and annoys me. I enjoy imagining that our two little ones have already arrived and are sleeping peacefully in their as-yet-unfinished nursery, but I also use this opportunity to survey the work to be done. I still have curtains and dust ruffles to make, pictures to frame, diapers and wipes to buy, and clothes to sort through.

Until yesterday, the two cribs stood side by side waiting for mattresses which are not budgeted until next month. For some reason, not having those mattresses has bugged me. As silly as it sounds, I have allowed worrying about this detail to rob me of some of my joy. Every time another person told me that twins *always* come early, my stomach would do a flip and my brow would furrow. I would think about the unfinished nursery and particularly those mattresses. "My babies would have nowhere to sleep," went my irrational thinking. Perhaps the hormonal surges of pregnancy have been getting to me, or maybe my natural tendency to get bogged down in the details of life has been kicking in, but certainly, I have been forgetting that God takes care of the small stuff, too.

Last night, we had just returned home from a long and tiring out-of-town trip. I was wearily picking up the fallout from our rushed departure that morning while Gene was unloading the car, carrying items from the garage back to our bedroom.

"When did you buy the mattresses?" asked Gene, walking back to get another load.

"What?" I replied.

"The baby mattresses. When did you buy those? And how in the world did you get them in the cribs?"

"I didn't," I said. Then the realization began to hit me. "Are there mattresses back there?"

Gene nodded. "Yup."

"Did you buy the mattresses to surprise me?" I was ready to give him a huge, thankful hug, wondering how in the world he could have smuggled in mattresses when he was with me the whole day.

"No. It wasn't me."

We walked down the hallway to the nursery. Sure enough, mattresses had "magically" appeared. They were exactly the ones we had planned to buy. For a brief moment, I felt like angels had dropped those mattresses from above. We couldn't imagine from where else they could have come. Their "miraculous" appearance was to me a reminder from God that he would take care of the details of life—that I didn't need to worry about the small stuff. Later we found out that my sister, Tina, had single-handedly purchased, transported, and installed those mattresses while we were gone. God used her to ease our stress, reminding us of his faithfulness.

Focusing on God's faithfulness is the only sane way to live. Worrying, even over the little things (maybe especially over the little things), makes us physically sick, irritable with our spouse, and generally miserable. Worrying robs us of valuable energy and paralyzes our ability to make choices and take action.

God has given us a way out of worry: prayer. Prayer sometimes changes our situation, sending us mattresses when we need them. Sometimes prayer only changes us, making us content with what we have. Either way, prayer works, giving us a taste of what we all want in this hectic, overloaded world—the peace of God.

God, thank you for a way out of worry. Teach us to trust in you so completely that our lives are filled with peace no matter what our situation.

QUIET MOMENTS

> MARK 4:35–41
> *Quiet! Be still!*
> *(v. 39).*

Living in Mississippi, we have numerous powerful thunderstorms and tornadoes. Often the proverbial calm before the storm warns us to be prepared for the impending tempest. Sandwiched between scorching heat and raging storm is a momentary interlude of peaceful coolness. The leaves on the trees make a wonderful hushed rippling, and the wind chimes on our back porch tinkle softly. We love to sit back and enjoy these brief moments before the violent storms come in, downing trees and damaging homes. In the midst of these awful storms, we sometimes think of the permeating quiet just a few moments before the storm and are encouraged that the peace will eventually return.

While playing golf the other day with my buddy Glenn, I was startled by his off-the-cuff comment: "You guys have pretty much had a prefect pregnancy, haven't you?"

Although I should have been thankful and happy, I was miserable for the rest of my round of golf because I kept thinking about how calm everything seemed to be. Lisa was healthy, and the sonograms showed babies developing normally. I wondered, *What if this is the calm before the storm? What could be coming after these lengthy quiet moments of "perfect pregnancy"?*

Jesus stood in that boat as the storm raged, and he commanded the tempest to cease. A delicious kind of peace overwhelmed the situation and eased the disciples' fears. In our pregnancy, we savor each calm day, realizing that the next may bring extra stresses or even unexpected health problems. We don't allow ourselves to grow anxious waiting for the potential crises; we savor the days that are without difficulties. A day without back pain is a blessing! Another day without being put on total bed rest is a gift from God! When things do spin out of control and the storms come, we must remember these quiet times that can help us find peace in the midst of our storms. Even a brief respite can be enough to sustain us through dark days.

> *Lord, grant us the proper perspective on the dark days of this life. Calm our superstitions and remind us who is truly the Lord of the storm.*

GIFTS

GIFT IDEAS

MATTHEW
7:9–11
*Which of you, if his
son asks for bread,
will give him a stone?
Or if he asks for a
fish, will give him a
snake?* (vv. 9–10).

Have you been to the baby gift registry kiosk at a department store yet? Our local stores have those scanner guns that you can use to shoot at the UPC price codes on the shelves and create a list of everything you could possibly need. When we registered for the first time, we were shooting up the whole store. It's the ultimate in window-shopping.

"The pregnancy manual says we'll need six of those," I would say.

"With twins, make it *twelve*," Gene would add.

By the time we finished, we had produced a ten-page wish list! We had everything from a double stroller to diaper pins. And the cute things! Oh what fun we had as we imagined our little ones in all sorts of outfits and contraptions.

We have already started thinking about the gifts *we* want to give our little ones, too. I have a baby ring, given to me by my dad's dad. One of our children will be the fifth generation to receive it. I had my wedding dress specially preserved and packed away so that if one day my daughter wanted to wear it, I could pass it on to her. Likewise, Gene has antique books that our children will inherit.

As special as these gifts are, however, our "gift registry" includes gifts of even greater value—like a home filled with

laughter, compassion, forgiveness, security, and encouragement. We realize our children will value these gifts much
longer than any toys we might give them. These gifts will be
heirlooms worth passing on to our children's children and to
their children's children.

While we may desire to give our children gifts from deep
within ourselves, we may not have a clear idea of how to
bestow these gifts. Perhaps we didn't receive these gifts ourselves as children, and certainly we struggle with sinful
natures that smother these good gifts in the daily grind of living.

This Scripture passage reminds us that God is our loving
heavenly Father who not only has great ideas for gifts but also
knows how to bestow those gifts on us. We can ask God to
instill these traits in us so that we might give them to our children.

If you could register your children for such gifts, what
would this wish list include? You may want to talk about what
gifts of lasting value you would like to give to your children,
and pray even now to be prepared when the opportunities
arise to pass on these good gifts.

*Heavenly Father, give us good gifts so that we may pass
them on to our children. Make us wise in our choices and
deliberate in our giving.*

THE GIFT OF COMPASSION

COLOSSIANS
3:12–14
*Clothe yourselves
with compassion,
kindness, humility,
gentleness and
patience (v. 12).*

The week my grandfather died I was able to provide him with a final act of love. He was in a nursing home following a stroke and a heart attack; his speech was garbled and his thinking confused. He mumbled huskily and tried to gesture, but the covers on the bed limited his range of motion. I could tell he was trying to communicate something to me and was becoming frustrated. I leaned closer to catch the hoarse words coming from his dry lips.

Finally, I determined that his feet were hot, so I pulled back the covers and took off his thick socks. The skin of his soles felt dry and papery. As I massaged his feet, he kept whispering over and over that his feet were on fire. He had a stack of paper towels on the small sink in his room, so I wet some with cool water and wrapped his feet in them. Almost immediately, he fell asleep, and Lisa and I slipped out of the room. That was the last time I saw him alive.

I think back on that natural act: caring for a loved one. I remember my mom's brothers and sisters taking turns caring for their parents after surgeries and strokes. On one occasion, Mom told us that her father hadn't been able to trim his toenails in several months. They were in horrible shape, yellowed and beginning to curl, a disgusting image to my fourteen-year-old's mind. I couldn't believe that anyone could touch such feet, yet Mom and her siblings took care of him. I guess that my cooling my grandfather's feet was an act that had been planted almost twenty years previously as I had observed my parents' selfless compassion.

Just as my parents instilled in me the importance of compassion, I want to pass this gift along to my own family. When I am tired at the end of a hard day now, I can practice compassion toward Lisa by massaging her swollen ankles and feet. One night in the future, when one of the children is up sick, I will need to forego sleep and provide the care needed. Modeling selflessness will teach my children to clothe themselves in patience, kindness, and humility so that they will be properly dressed for meeting the heartlessness of the world with the love and hope that Christ offers.

Father, make us sensitive to the needs around us; make us compassionate, kind, and patient so that our children will be the same.

THE GIFT OF ENCOURAGEMENT

> **PROVERBS 12:25**
> *An anxious heart weighs a man down, but a kind word cheers him up.*

My parents had a friend, Billy Rogers, who was a great encourager. Each day, he set aside time to write brief notes to family, friends, and associates. Billy's habit grew so prodigious, in fact, that his family members would give him stationery and postage stamps for Christmas each year. He had such a gift with words that with just a few lines, he could shore up sagging self-esteems, empower consciences to do right, and fortify crumbling hope in a letter's recipient.

My parents have told me that there were several occasions where Billy's notes were timed almost supernaturally. When they were home missionaries, a note from Billy would always seem to arrive during difficult times. Mom and Dad would see that return address on the envelope and smile immediately, for they knew that it would contain cheerful words of encouragement.

Billy's correspondence left its mark on people all over the world who have saved stacks of his notes, wrapped them in bits of ribbon, and stashed them somewhere in their personal belongings. In our travels, Lisa and I have met dozens of people who don't know each other but who have sheaves of letters from this dear saint.

As I think over the things we want to give our children, unwavering encouragement is near the top of the list. What a precious gift to give! Encouragement, meaning, literally, "to give heart to," is the antidote for disheartenment. The world will dish out plenty of bitterness and cynicism to our children, overwhelming them with frustration and disheartenment. As parents, we will need to become experts at giving our children heart in a discouraging world.

Are you an inveterate encourager? If you're not practicing giving this gift now with your spouse, you probably won't practice it with your children either. How long has it been since you slipped a note into your spouse's briefcase on a day that you know will be particularly difficult for her? When was the last time you went out of your way to say to your spouse, "You work so hard! Thanks!" You may be surprised at how your efforts will encourage you as well.

Lord, make us encouragers who fight against the negativity that so permeates our world. Help us to be examples from whom our little ones can learn to give heart to others.

THE GIFT OF SECURITY

My nesting instinct kicked in early, and I became increasingly stressed that our little ones' room was not ready. One Saturday I marshaled the troops: my sister, Tina, painted over the scribbled walls in the closet, and Gene painted an old chest of drawers and the two used cribs we had purchased. I supervised from afar, not wanting to risk exposing the babies to the paint fumes. I was beginning to feel more prepared. We had a place for our children to sleep and a place to store their belongings.

But something was missing. Although we had the bare necessities, I couldn't get the idea of a rocker out of my mind. I have fond memories of being rocked as a young child in my grandmother's gooseneck rocker. There is something so wonderfully secure, so comforting about rocking. So many people had told me how helpful a baby swing would be, and I thought that perhaps we should spend our money on that instead, but how could we have a baby's room without a rocking chair? I knew in my heart that a mechanical device can't take the place of being held by someone who thinks you are the apple of her eye and broods over you like a hen with her chicks.

Occasionally I still long for the comfort of being rocked, and I like to think of my heavenly Father holding me in his arms, giving me the confidence that I am loved and cared for. Eventually, I did buy an old-fashioned rocker for the nursery, one that was within our price range and nearly matched the picture in my mind's eye. We look forward to giving our little ones a taste of that nurturing security that they can experience as beloved children of God.

Father, thank you for treating us as favored children, protected by your love. May we remember your example as we care for our children.

THE GIFT OF LAUGHTER

> ## PROVERBS
> ### 15:15
> *The cheerful heart has a continual feast.*

One of our friends has a two-year-old who hasn't yet learned how to think without talking out loud. His compulsion to speak almost constantly causes some pretty interesting moments around the house, especially at bedtime. He gets in his bed and retells to himself the events of the day: "We went to Grandma's house today and saw ducks, and a cow, and we ate peanut butter sandwiches, and then we fished. . . ." Well, you get the idea. What's really cute, though, is when he thinks of something funny; he will repeat the incident or the joke to himself again and again, giggling uncontrollably the entire time. Soon his mom and dad are giggling as well. Children's laughter is so contagious.

A home filled with laughter is a satisfying place to be. I am blessed to have an Uncle Ray, whose corny jokes cause everyone to roll their eyes, a Cousin Christy, whose story-telling puts everyone in stitches, and an Uncle Buddy, whose hearty laughter is contagious. When we all get together, our hearts do indeed have a feast of good cheer.

In the Middle Ages, a tradition developed regarding the belief that Christ never smiled or laughed. We have a hard time believing that Christ didn't partake in the feasts of laughter at the wedding in Cana or out on the fishing boat with the disciples.

As we lie in bed together, we often swap the humorous incidents of the day, funny emails, unlikely student excuses for late assignments, cartoon clippings, jokes we heard. Our babies share in our bedtime ritual, as Lisa shakes and jostles them in laughter. Certainly they hear her chuckles from the inside. When they are born in a few short weeks, we want them to recognize our laughs as well as our voices. We look forward to them filling our home with their contagious giggles.

Father, make our family joyful. Fill us with the easy laughter that comes from persons who love each other and enjoy being together.

THE GIFT OF A SERVANT'S HEART

JOHN 13:1–17
*Now that I, your
Lord and Teacher,
have washed your
feet, you also should
wash one another's
feet. I have set you an
example that you
should do as I have
done for you
(vv. 14–15).*

Anyone who is around me for very long will hear stories about my adventures with Steve Gooding, better known as "Pood." He has given me material for more stories and anecdotes than anyone else from my adolescence; most of my students could tell you a Pood story even though they have never met him. All of us who know Pood can agree on one thing: he has always had a servant's heart. If I needed help at 4 A.M., I could call on him. If my car broke down three hours away from home, he'd come. He might not have known how to fix what needed repairing, but he was always happy to help me, and boy, did we have fun. His heart is as big as that of anyone I have ever known.

I wish that I had more of a servant's heart. More times than not, I am in my own little world, worrying about myself and ignoring those around me. A good example of this is our evening meal; meal preparation has become the hardest part of our day. I often leave work and forget to call Lisa to see how she's doing or if she needs me to pick up anything for her. Sometimes she calls right when I am leaving and asks me to pick up supper on the way home, but many times she misses me, and we have to opt for cold cereal instead of going through the hassle of cooking.

On those nights when I feel like grumbling about a meager dinner, it helps me to remember this passage. I am learning that there are times when I need to do the hard, menial tasks. I need to lift up my eyes from my own selfish concerns and take care of Lisa's needs.

When we cultivate a servant's heart, we actually are reworking our priorities. We are placing the needs of others ahead of our own selfish desires. We act from a desire to help others out of love and concern. We go out of our way to allow our actions to edify our loved ones. Amazingly, I always feel better about myself when I put others' needs above my own because I have looked beyond my own narrow little perspective on the world.

God has given everyone talents and abilities. Perhaps the most overlooked gift is that of simple service. Christ humbled himself to demonstrate that no act of service is too lowly. His message applies in the home as well. Someone has to scrub the toilet and the bathtub grout. Laundry has to be done. Someone will have to get up at 3 A.M. and change a really stinky diaper or mop up vomit. When we demonstrate a servant's heart to our children, we are teaching them, just as Christ taught us.

Lord, make us willing to serve others faithfully and tirelessly; instill servant's hearts in our children.

THE GIFT OF FORGIVENESS

In one of my favorite episodes of *Leave It to Beaver,* Mrs. Cleaver breaks up a fight between Wally and the Beav and demands that they apologize to each other. Begrudgingly the two boys apologize, but soon begin fighting again, much to their mother's exasperation. By nightfall, though, she observes the brothers working on a project together in spite of their obviously hollow exchange of apologies. Wise Ward explains to June that while the boys may not have sincerely apologized to each other, they had forgiven each other.

Our lives are hardly like black-and-white sitcoms. We are pretty good arguers by nature, and both Lisa and I hate to lose.

"You never told me that you wanted me to hang those shelves in the nursery," I'll say.

"No, you never *heard* me say that," I'll hear Lisa say in return. "You never hear what I say. At least listen to me when we are talking about the babies' room!"

After a few more exchanges like those we will figure out that both of us probably didn't communicate very well, and we apologize to each other. Sometimes, though, that apology takes a while to sink in. It's so easy to keep our frustrations with one another in a secret file of some sort, ready to be brought out later when we can use the extra ammunition in another argument about something completely different. We may have said the words "I'm sorry," but we really haven't forgiven the incident.

So often we put an emphasis on words of apology when instead we need to focus on forgiveness. In marriage, we will often apologize, but it's much more difficult to forgive a wrong. God has loved us and forgiven us, freeing us to love and forgive one another.

As we teach our children, we hope to give them the gift of forgiving. One day, we as parents may need to receive forgiveness from them! (I seem to remember another episode of *Beaver* where Ward has to apologize to the boys; what a great show.) Hopefully our children will have learned from us and from Ephesians 4:32 that we need to be kind and compassionate; we need to forgive one another.

Father, remind us to forgive one another as you have forgiven us. Make us tenderhearted.

RESOURCES

WE CAN'T AFFORD TO HAVE CHILDREN!

> ### LUKE 12:29–31
> *And do not set your heart on what you will eat or drink; do not worry about it. For the pagan world runs after all such things, and your Father knows that you need them. But seek his kingdom, and these things will be given to you as well.*

The first time we decided to peek at some baby clothes at the mall was too early in the pregnancy to buy anything, but those cute little outfits were irresistible. We were having such a good time admiring all of the little hats and coats, socks and shoes, dresses and overalls, trying to imagine what our little ones would look like in them. Our conversation was sprinkled with phrases like, "Look, how cute!" "Oh, that one's precious!" "Won't she be an angel in this one?" "Won't our little man be adorable in this?" Our fun, however, soon turned to dismay as we began to examine price tags (and multiply by two). If you have not looked at baby clothes yet, you're in for a little sticker shock. We left the store feeling a little deflated at the inflated prices of children's clothes.

Clothes aren't the only items needed for a new baby. A layette includes diapers and wipes, towels and washcloths, sheets and blankets. Our babies could go through some 5,000 diapers their first year; if we choose to use formula, add another $4,000. What about the hospital costs, the doctor's visits, the nursery furniture, the strollers, the car seats, the toys, the clothes, and the unknown incidentals that seem to come out of nowhere? Every time we look at our budget, we are overwhelmed by tension and anxiety. How will we afford all of these expenses, especially since I won't be able to return to work for a while?

We keep reminding ourselves that we've been in training for this situation through six years of graduate school and three-and-a-half years of medical bills for infertility treatments. The last nine years were just a warm-up for this big test: surviving on less money with more mouths to feed.

Faith is in some ways an exercise in walking backwards. We face our past, looking at how God has provided for us, and step into the future with confidence, blind to what is ahead. One of our favorite faith markers of the past is our ten-year-old Ford Festiva. Although it is little more than a stripped-down roller skate with no air-conditioning (a real inconvenience in the long, hot, humid Mississippi summers) and a radio that changes its own stations, it is probably the best car we've ever owned.

The Festiva came into our life at a time when we desperately needed a second vehicle. Gene was commuting from New Orleans to Hattiesburg, Mississippi, to work on his doctorate. He would leave on Mondays and return on Fridays. Because I worked outside the city limits, I was out of the range of public transportation and without the benefit of a car pool. I needed a car, but we had no idea how we would afford a second car on my teaching salary, so we began to pray. We are convinced that God led us to this used but spunky, bright blue Festiva. It was highly dependable, cheap to maintain and insure, got great gas mileage (perfect for Gene's long commute), compact (great for parking on campus), and miraculously within our budgetary constraints. Wow, God! Thanks. When we think about the Festiva, we know God will provide for our children. God gave us these

little ones, and he will make sure their needs are met. He cares for those he loves.

Almost everyone feels overwhelmed by the cost of absorbing another person into the family budget. Pregnancies are not always planned, and they are not always financially feasible, but God specializes in infeasibilities. When you place your trust in him, he will not disappoint you. You may want to try some "backwards faith walking" by talking about the times God has provided for your needs in the past. You will be assured of his care for you in the future.

Father, help us to remember that you love us and will provide for us. Remind us to put you first, trusting in your faithfulness.

GADGET MANIA

ECCLESIASTES
2:1–11
*I denied myself noth-
ing my eyes
desired.... Yet when I
surveyed all that my
hands had done and
what I had toiled to
achieve, everything
was meaningless, a
chasing after the
wind; nothing was
gained under the sun
(vv. 10–11).*

As we shop for baby items, we are amazed at how many gadgets and devices are "necessary"—and how expensive most of them are. How on earth do women living in the garbage dumps in Mexico function without video surveillance monitors? How do parents who live in the sandy Kalahari Desert survive without a super-rugged baby buggy with oversized tires and a customized suspension system to cushion bumps? What did our mothers do without special "saucers" for exercise, disposable diapers, and electric baby wipe warmers? How did Einstein develop his genius without those stimulating black, white, and red infant toys?

It's so easy to get caught up in the material drive with these little ones. So many of these seemingly useful gadgets are awfully appealing. Since we want to be the best parents we can be, shouldn't we buy the things our precious children need to have a good start in life? After all, our kids are going to be the cutest and smartest ones ever. Don't they deserve the best of everything?

We find ourselves constantly evaluating our spending. Is that item *really* necessary, or could we buy more diapers with that money? We hope our spending habits aren't teaching our babies to be materialistic while they are still in the womb. We want them to appreciate how God has blessed us beyond measure. Our chasing after material things, no matter how fashionable they are or how necessary they seem, only diminishes his place at the center of our lives.

Father, help us to remember the real purpose for material things: accomplishing a task or helping others, not showing others how cute our babies are or how successful we are as parents. Help us to keep you at the center of our lives.

BABY SHOWERS OF BLESSINGS

> **EZEKIEL 34:25–31**
>
> *I will bless them and the places surrounding my hill. I will send down showers in season; there will be showers of blessing (v. 26).*

When Gene was in graduate school, God taught us a valuable lesson in gratitude. I began keeping a "provision journal." Some people call them gratitude journals. The journal was nothing more than a list of ways that God had provided for our needs. Items on the list included anything from actual monies we received (gifts, rebates, refunds, scholarships, and loans) to material items that were given, loaned, or purchased at a reduced price to wages we received from freelance work opportunities (writing, teaching, speaking, etc.). Sometimes these provisions were given to us so that we could pay a bill. Sometimes a provision allowed us to go out on a date—a luxury on our budget. Sometimes the money was provided so that we could experience the joy of giving it back to the Lord's work or to someone else.

We were amazed at how quickly our list grew to be unmanageable. The more we thought about specific provisions for which to be thankful, the more our eyes were opened to ways that God had indeed provided. We had just never stopped to notice before. Keeping track of blessings in this way changed our attitude about our finances in several ways: we began to focus on all that we had rather than what we did not have; we realized more than ever that God would provide what we needed when we needed it; and we were filled with gratitude to him and to all of the people he used to bless us.

Now that we are pregnant, our hearts are full of gratitude again as we watch him prepare for our little ones' arrival. From free car seats provided by the hospital to equipment borrowed from friends, our children's needs are being met before our very eyes. We are blessed to have a Mothers of Multiples Club that sponsors a sale of secondhand items twice a year. We bought cribs and other equipment at a fraction of the cost of new items. My mom, who has a knack for finding treasures at yard sales and thrift stores, has been stocking up on clothes for our babies. Junk mail has become fun as we are thankful for those manufacturers' promotions that bombard our mailbox with coupons for diapers, wipes, and diaper ointment. Friends have begun clipping coupons and sending us addresses to write for free baby stuff. Family members with older children have promised hand-me-downs, and then people have poured out blessing after blessing at baby showers. We are humbled with gratitude to God for the material blessings and for the people who have participated in our joy by providing for our little ones!

Spending some time together counting your blessings is time well-spent. Even if things seem bleak right now, make the effort to look for ways that God has provided for you either by giving you the opportunity to work or through the generosity of others.

Father, give us a heart full of gratitude. Thank you for meeting our needs; bless those who have blessed us so much.

DECISIONS

JOEL 3:14–16
Multitudes, multitudes in the valley of decision! . . . But the LORD will be a refuge for his people, a stronghold for the people of Israel (vv. 14, 16).

A troubling side effect of pregnancy has been my inability to make decisions. I returned our new bedspread three times because I was haunted by the other options back at the store. Choosing fabric for the nursery has been a nightmare! Now that I am steadily outgrowing my smaller-sized maternity clothes, I dread making a decision about what to wear every morning. How can I be expected to make major decisions like whether to go back to work after the baby is born and, if so, should it be part time or full time?

You may not have a choice about returning to work, but if you do have a choice, chances are it is not an easy one. Husbands and wives may not see eye to eye on this issue, making it a source of quarreling during an already tense period of life. Many couples we know changed their minds several times before the pregnancy was over and several more times before the end of maternity leave.

The valley of decision is sometimes a bleak place (notice that it's not called the mountaintop of decision). In a valley, you cannot see what is ahead—what is on the other side of the mountain—and you tend to lose sight of what is behind. All you can see is the decision. God, however, does not see things from the valley; he sees the entire picture—past, present, and future. He is our stronghold in the vulnerable valley of decision. As we make difficult decisions, he offers us the refuge of his loving wisdom and providential care.

Lord, help us as we anguish over tough choices; reveal your wisdom to us.

GENEROSITY

> ## LUKE 21:1–4
> *"I tell you the truth,"* he said, *"this poor widow has put in more than all the others. All these people gave their gifts out of their wealth; but she out of her poverty put in all she had to live on"* (vv. 3–4).

I worked at the University of Southern Mississippi when the now-famous gift was made by Osceola McCarty. You may have read about this marvelous woman who worked for her entire lifetime as a laundry woman, never owning a car or an air conditioner or many clothes. She endowed a scholarship fund of over $150,000 for the university. The morning of the announcement, I asked the president of the university, Dr. Aubrey Lucas, if this gift wasn't the most amazing one he had seen during his long tenure. He paused for a moment and commented, "It should make those of us who have so many blessings really stop and think and maybe be ashamed with how we spend our money."

Never before in our married life have we been so aware of our financial situation. It seems as though all of our resources are going toward doctors' bills and baby necessities. Increasingly we find ourselves tempted to quench the spirit of generosity by cutting back on our church tithe and the other charities we support. We look at those checks each month and are tempted by the thought of how *we* could use that money in spite of the commitments we have made to these other groups.

Does the story of the widow's mite trouble you? We can certainly go back into our old check registers and find entries that make us feel a bit ashamed. If our children go through these old registers one day, what will stand out to them as our highest priorities in spending? Will our tithe checks be noticeable? What would such an inspection teach your children? Our actions clearly illustrate our priorities, especially where our little ones are concerned. If we think and plan ahead, we will be able to look back one day and say with confidence that not only were we responsible with our blessings but we also taught our children to be the same.

Lord, make us good stewards of your blessings. Give us opportunities to teach our little ones about giving and about your sacrificial gift of salvation.

TIME MANAGEMENT

Are you one of those people who keeps a list of things to do? Both of us keep lists that help us plan ahead and keep track of the details of daily life. It's pretty amazing how those lists keep getting longer even though we keep checking items off each day. Where does the time go? How can we get everything done when that due date gets closer every day?

I was speaking the other day with a coworker, the father of a one-year-old, about time frustrations. Neither of us felt like we were juggling the demands of fatherhood very well. My to-do lists had overwhelmed me, and he was discouraged about not spending time with his daughter. We came to this realization: time is the only human resource that is truly fixed. You can't buy more time, steal it, or get more on credit (at least the government hasn't figured out how to tax it yet!).

Frequently, we feel like we have little time for each other between work, family obligations, and daily chores like doing the laundry, fixing meals, maintaining the house and the cars, taking care of the cat—the list of tasks is endless. With children added to the equation, how can we accomplish it all?

When can we ever go on dates again with our spouses or take leisurely naps on Sunday afternoon? It's all a bit overwhelming.

We have a saying in our household: "cleaning chandeliers." We used to rent a townhouse that had a small light fixture that vaguely resembled a chandelier. At the time Lisa had a huge project she was responsible for at work, and whenever deadlines were looming for her projects, she would get on a chair and buff up that fixture. It was her way of feeling "useful" while respectably procrastinating. Of course, the problem with cleaning the chandeliers is that we really find ourselves even more behind in spite of our "busyness."

Time is a valuable resource; we must be good stewards of this asset. The commandment recorded in Exodus teaches us that we can more effectively manage the time we are given by following God's design. We all have more things to do than time to do them, but God commands us to take time out to worship him and to rest. Though it's easier said than done, time management is a matter of priorities. What is *really* important? Does our postponement of tasks or misplacing of priorities only make us more pressured and frustrated? God is an expert in time management. If we follow his design, we will find ourselves more organized and more able to deal with the demands on our time.

Father, remind us that you are the Lord of the Sabbath, and that we must take time to rest, reflect, and prepare for the days that lie ahead of us.

SATISFACTION

JAMES 4:1–3

What causes fights and quarrels among you? Don't they come from your desires that battle within you? You want something but don't get it. You kill and covet, but you cannot have what you want. You quarrel and fight. You do not have, because you do not ask God. When you ask, you do not receive, because you ask with wrong motives, that you may spend what you get on your pleasures.

A friend of ours, Ted, drove a terrible junk car. It was noisy and dented, and he hated driving it despite its absolute reliability, but he simply could not afford another vehicle. Another friend, Warren, drove a beautiful blue Cadillac, shiny and equipped with every conceivable option. Warren kept that car immaculate, washing it every Saturday.

Ted wished that he could have such a nice car. One day he quipped to Warren, "Boy, it must be nice to have such a beautiful, comfortable car."

"It is," Warren replied. "But I'd rather still have my mom alive. She left it to me when she died of cancer."

In his ignorance of Warren's situation, Ted had allowed his sense of dissatisfaction to make him feel less valuable; he was looking at Warren's car and asking himself, "Why him and not me?" He didn't know the true cost of Warren's car.

Lisa and I find ourselves looking around a great deal lately. Other couples who are expecting a baby seem to have less of a struggle with their finances than we do. Some don't appear to be agonizing over whether the wife will return to work full time or not. Occasionally these "observations" really get us depressed and dissatisfied.

Satisfaction with our state in life says a great deal about our relationship with God. When our primary focus is on God, our satisfaction lies in him and his grace. When our focus rests on our accumulation of "stuff" or our relationships with others, our dissatisfactions are many. James's statement concerning covetousness still applies; why are we so unhappy? God gives us what we need, and it all belongs to him: finances, time, energy, health, everything. Blessed be the name of the Lord!

Father, you bless us in ways that we fail to remember. Refresh our minds with the satisfaction that comes from knowing that you love us and care for us and that our value comes from our relationship with you, not from our collection of resources.

SPIRITUAL
LESSONS

LESSON ONE:
God Loves Me

> ISAIAH 49:15–16
>
> *Can a mother forget the baby at her breast and have no compassion on the child she has borne? Though she may forget, I will not forget you! See, I have engraved you on the palms of my hands.*

As expectant parents, we already grasp the beauty of Isaiah's word picture more fully than before the pregnancy. What a beautiful image a nursing mother is, her baby's warm body pressed up close, pink cheeks bobbing to the sound of satisfied gulping and swallowing. Attending childbirth classes has started me thinking about our children's complete dependency on us. We will provide them with all the basic human needs: food, clothing, shelter, security, and love. As a nursing mother, I will be their single source of nutrition; I will nurture them as I have never nurtured another human being. Although Gene and I both feel a little apprehensive and overwhelmed by the responsibility of taking care of a helpless, fragile newborn, we cannot imagine neglecting our beloved little ones' needs. This bond that already ties us to our children is the strongest on earth.

God's love and concern for us is even stronger. While Isaiah conveys the tender quality of the relationship between a woman and a child, other Scriptures provide illustrations of the loving father. Both parental relationships are used as metaphors for God's intimate relationship with humankind. As we confront the reality of becoming parents, we are just beginning to glimpse the deep meanings of these metaphors. We realize that parenthood will add a new dimension to our spiritual life, helping us to understand God's immeasurable love for us.

> *God, thank you for teaching us through our experience of becoming parents that you will never forget us. Remind us that no matter how much we love our little ones, your love for them and for us is even stronger.*

LESSON TWO:
God Speaks

JOHN 10:1–18
I am the good shepherd; I know my sheep and my sheep know me (v. 14).

At bedtime we enjoy talking to the babies. I put my face over Lisa's belly and yell tenderly, "We love you two! We can't wait to see you!" Sometimes I tell jokes to them, trying to stimulate a sense of humor early on. Lisa says she feels like the speaker box at a drive-through restaurant window. When our parents call, Lisa lies next to the speakerphone so the babies can hear their grandparents tell us what's going on back home. Many nights, I pray loudly so that the little ones can hear me.

We wonder what the little ones think when they hear these noises through the womb's waters. Although they cannot understand what is said or from where the voices come, our children surely sense our love for them, wiggling and kicking in response to us. Imagine what babies must think, then, when in the delivery room they can actually see the faces that belong to those voices they've been hearing. Doctors say that newborns will actually turn their heads and look in the direction of their parents' voices. We can't wait to see if that happens with ours!

God speaks to us; we don't know exactly how, but he makes known to us his will and his ways. We can't see him, and we can't explain the means of communication he uses, but we can sense his love for us. One day, we will hear our shepherd's voice and meet him face-to-face. On that day, if we have trained our ears to listen, we will easily recognize his voice.

God, may your voice be familiar to us and to our children. Give us ears of faith that allow us to hear you speak to us.

LESSON THREE:
I Am God's Child

COLOSSIANS
1:15-22
*He is the image of
the invisible God,
the firstborn over
all creation (v. 15).*

When we were dating, we used to enjoy looking at old pictures together. One of my favorites was of Gene at about age three, wearing a little jacket and bow tie. I loved this picture because it showed the characteristic openmouthed smile, with eyes turned up and twinkling, that I had come to love. Gene once told me that if I married him, I could have children that looked like that picture. Although his comment might have sounded a bit conceited, I couldn't deny that I would love to have a little one with that smile. At our wedding reception, next to my bridal portrait, we displayed copies of that picture and one of me at about the same age.

Now that we're expecting, we look at some of those old pictures and try to imagine what our little ones will look like. We even scan our sonogram images, trying to decipher the details of those delicate profiles. Do they have Gene's smile or my hair? Will their eyes be blue, like Gene's, or green, like mine? Whose temperament will they have? Will they be bold and gregarious or quiet and reserved? Will they be night owls like their dad or early birds like their mom? The desire to see ourselves in the next generation must be universal. We would probably be disappointed if our children did not bear some resemblance to us, for that is their emblem of being ours. We would certainly be heartbroken if they did not share our values as they grow older.

God himself created Adam and Eve in his image, but their sin marred the manifestation of his glory. God restored his beloved creation through his Son, the firstborn of creation and the perfect human image of the invisible God. Through Jesus Christ, God looks at us as his "little spittin' images"; there is no doubt that we are his own because the resemblance is clear. Just as we long to have a close relationship with our offspring, he desires to have an intimate relationship with each of us. When we recognize God's image in us as it has been restored through Christ, we cannot help but desire an intimate relationship with him.

Father, we thank you for imprinting your image in us as a sign of your devotion. Remind us that others learn about you through our reflection of your love.

LESSON FOUR:
God Is with Me

> PSALM 139:1–12
> *Where can I go from your Spirit? Where can I flee from your presence? (v. 7).*

I am now in the seventh month of pregnancy. There is not a time of any day or night when I am not aware of the babies. When I lie down to rest, I feel their vigorous movements in my belly and my back. When I roll over, I'm restricted by their shifting weight. When I eat, my almost insatiable appetite reflects their nutritional needs. When I climb stairs, my racing heartbeat echoes their two tiny ones. When I embrace my husband, their bodies intervene. I have grown accustomed to their presence, and I sometimes think that after they are born, I will miss having them with me all of the time.

My father-in-law has reminded me that in the same way, God's presence is with us always. Sometimes he gives us joy; sometimes he restrains us; sometimes he intervenes in our relationships; but always, he is here with us.

In his psalm, David was awestruck by the omnipresence of God. He recognized that even if he had wanted to get away from the presence of the Almighty, he could not have. Finding a place where God is not is an impossibility. He is present at the beginning of a life; he will be present at the end; and he knows every thought and deed in between.

Wouldn't it be wonderful if we could recognize God's presence in our lives with the same awareness that a pregnant woman has of her babies in the womb? Whether we recognize his presence or not doesn't change the fact of that presence, of course, but God created us to live in the most intimate of relationships with him. Surely he desires that we live every moment, knowing he is at hand.

Lord, make us sensitive to the presence of your Spirit in our lives. Restore to us the joy of knowing that you never leave us.

LESSON FIVE:
God Is Constant

> **HEBREWS 13:8**
> *Jesus Christ is the same yesterday and today and forever.*

One thing we have decided about pregnancy: no two days are the same. One day Lisa feels like Supermom, and the next she can barely get out of bed. One day I am depressed about the upcoming hospital bills; the next I'm elated over becoming a father. At night we spend a good part of our conversation going over these ups and downs and trying to make sense of them.

If we had our way, every day would be a good day. There would be no mood swings, no new aches, and no unexpected bills. We would get up in the morning feeling rested and go through our day feeling vigorous and productive. At night we would chat in bed about the day's events and fall asleep with easy smiles on our faces. The next day would be the same. It would be a bit like a summer weather forecast in South Mississippi or a winter forecast in the Upper Peninsula of Michigan: yesterday was the same as today, and tomorrow will keep the same pattern.

The trouble with such a wish is that it is not very realistic; in fact, it is almost cartoonish. In this world we ride a roller coaster of good days and bad, aches and ecstasies, grief and joy. This truth prevails not only in pregnancy but in all of life. This life is transient, and everything in it is bound to that rule of change; however, remembering that Christ is eternally the same can ease the frustrations of these earthly extremes. When we have aches, he is Christ, and when we have ecstasies, he remains Christ. In both our grief and in our joy, he is still Christ.

God, help us in this ever-changing world to find comfort in the changelessness of Jesus Christ. Remind us that you are ever-present in our lives.

LESSON SIX:
We Are God's Family

ACTS 2:42–47

All the believers were together and had everything in common.... They broke bread in their homes and ate together with glad and sincere hearts, praising God and enjoying the favor of all the people. And the Lord added to their number daily those who were being saved

(*vv. 44, 46–47*).

Our Sunday school class, unbelievably, has had eight pregnancies (most of them first-time pregnancies) this year! The conversations each week are pleasantly predictable: "Have you felt the babies kick yet?" "When do you go for the next sonogram?" "What are you doing with your nursery?" Although we may have very different interests, backgrounds, and lifestyles, our pregnancies have given us a common bond.

In fact, now that I look unmistakably pregnant, I find that just about any woman I meet who has already had a child or who is pregnant has lots to talk to me about. Cashiers, shoppers, colleagues, and students all speak my language, the language of pregnancy. They ask questions, share stories, and contribute well wishes. The neighbors wave more often, and my friends call more often. People are more generous, as well, offering to share equipment, baby clothes, and maternity wear. This single aspect of my life, pregnancy, has created a commonality between me and so many different people. I must admit that life is much easier with all of this friendliness and encouragement; I wish people were like this all of the time.

The bond that we've felt with other expectant couples has made us think about the fellowship we should find in the church. The early church experienced a tremendous unity, worshiping, fellowshiping, and sharing with one another every day. Barriers of culture, language, and class were nullified by the common experience of believing in Christ.

We have a common bond, an adopted kinship, with those who are Christians. We should desire to fellowship with them, encouraging those who are going through what we have gone through and encouraged by those who have gone before us. Like the pregnant couples in my Sunday school class, we should compare notes about our experience of faith (give testimonies) and share our material resources with those in need.

When we express this sense of community, it will affect the world around us. What can be more attractive in a cynical, lonely world than an open community of believers who are friendly, supportive, and loving. It's no wonder the early church grew so quickly. When we live our lives in accordance with the love of Christ, our fellowship cannot help but grow.

Lord, thank you for the community of faith. Help us to love one another and encourage those who are around us, whether they are believers or have not yet come to know you.

LESSON SEVEN:
God Is in Control

> ## PROVERBS
> ### 16:1–4
> *To man belong the plans of the heart, but from the LORD comes the reply of the tongue. All a man's ways seem innocent to him, but motives are weighed by the LORD. Commit to the LORD whatever you do, and your plans will succeed. The LORD works out everything for his own ends.*

While sight-seeing in Bristol, Tennessee, we found ourselves on a gravel road that ran along the side of a mountain ridge overlooking a reservoir. Gene is terribly afraid of heights, and the drop of the ridge was several hundred feet, straight down into water. Even I was getting nervous at the precariousness of the situation; one slightly missed curve and we would be over the edge. I just couldn't believe that Gene wasn't white-knuckled, and I said, "Why aren't you scared?"

"Because," he said, "I'm the one driving. I'm in control. If you were driving, I'd be shivering on the floorboard. If we go over the edge, it's my fault, and I trust myself."

Perhaps the most important lesson we've learned in the last year has been how little control we have over so much of our lives. We both are plotters and planners. We set out our plans for our lives after high school and pursued our dreams, many of which were, quite frankly, self-centered. In spite of our elaborate planning, however, neither of us has the career we as teenagers had expected to pursue. We are farther in distance from beloved family members, we drive older cars, and we live in a much different house from what we had imagined. Yet we are happy because we believe that we are where we are because we have sought after God's will; we have tried to commit all of our plans to his control.

Pregnancy has been our supreme lesson in accepting God's control over every aspect of our lives. We know so many couples who were shocked to find out that they were expecting; they did "everything" right, and still had a little one on the way. Of course, we were the opposite: we had done "everything" right and had to wait nine years before these little ones were given to us. In either case, we are reminded that ultimately, in a way that we do not completely understand, God is in control.

Our efforts to wrest control from him and take charge for ourselves leave us in the same situation I would have encountered had I grabbed the steering wheel away from Gene on that mountain road: a terrible wreck. Our lives run smoother, our blood pressure lower, and our stress levels more even-keeled when we realize who is in control. We need to plan. We need to evaluate our lives and dream of the future, but we also need to remember that we really don't have much control over the world around us. The wise Lord of the universe, however, does.

Lord, we give control over to you. Hear our pleas, our dreams, and our hopes, but shape the desires of our hearts, so that we can obey your calling in our lives.

PARENTING

BABY DEDICATION

We received a package in the mail, our first baby gifts, from Mike and Peggy, a special couple who have been our friends and mentors for several years now. Inside the package were two gift boxes containing crisp, white cotton bibs with embroidered white crosses to be worn at a christening or baby dedication. Later we received other gifts also intended for this occasion: little white cotton outfits and Bibles from Lisa's parents, and bonnets, booties, and blankets from other dear friends. Each time we opened another of these gifts, we found that their simple beauty and symbolic importance impressed us with the awesome responsibility of our children's spiritual upbringing.

Our church is large, so several Sundays a month we have baby dedications at the end of the morning services. During these ceremonies, parents hold their children in the view of everyone while the church prays for the child's spiritual dedication to God. More importantly, perhaps, is the prayer of dedication for the parents and the church family to be responsible in their upbringing of the child. The baby dedication is not simply a dedication of the *child* to God, but a dedication of *ourselves* to God to train up the child he has given us.

We look forward to our little ones wearing their special outfits on that important day in our family's life. These gifts already have reminded us that our children are loaned to us, and we are called to be good stewards of God's trust. We will be the primary channels through which they will learn of and experience God's love. What an important charge and what a great privilege!

Hannah certainly understood her obligation as a parent; God had given her the special desire of her heart, and she returned the act of grace with an act of faith. Look at how her son Samuel influenced the lives of leaders like Saul and David. Samuel was God's prophet, who anointed kings and lived a life of devotion. He spoke the truth of God's word and urged others to follow God's will. Samuel's place in history was possible because of his mother's willingness to dedicate herself *and* her son to the Lord.

God, help us to remember that our children are also your children. Assist us as we endeavor to be responsible stewards of your trust.

PERFECT PARENTING

How many books, articles, seminars, and Internet chat rooms are there on successful parenting? Next to the Bible, Dr. Spock's baby book is the best-selling nonfiction book of all time. As parents we want to do our best; we want to do everything right. Certainly when it comes to being perfect parents, the pressure is on.

Our Sunday school teacher, who also is a family therapist, recently discussed the importance of realizing that we all are ultimately insufficient; only Christ is sufficient. His sufficiency and perfection are what give us hope. When we obsess over impossible perfection, we waste our time and energies. Embracing our weaknesses enables Christ's power to make us strong. How liberating to understand that we don't have to meet anyone's definition of perfection—that we are insufficient. The pressure is off!

In talking about parenting the other day, Gene meant to say that we were going to be "insufficient" parents, but instead he said that we would be "incompetent." Maybe that's even more correct! Obviously we don't mean that we will be willfully negligent or bumbling in our roles as parents, but no matter how hard we strive to be the best parents who ever lived, we constantly will fall short and fail from time to time. We even will need to apologize to our children once in a while. We will be totally imperfect parents, and that will be perfectly fine as long as we rely on Christ to fill in the gaps in our shortcomings.

God, help us to realize our limitations as parents. Give us the wisdom to know that we cannot be perfect, but that we can rely on your strength.

A QUIVER FULL

When I was a little girl, I loved hearing about large families. Perhaps because I was an only child for so long (I was almost eleven when my sister, Tina, was born, fourteen when Dana came along, and graduating from high school the week Ryan was born!), books like *Cheaper by the Dozen* and television shows like *The Waltons, Eight Is Enough,* and *The Brady Bunch* intrigued me. These fictional families seemed to have so much fun, with children running all over the place and their parents taking mishaps in stride. Although I know that these depictions were romanticized versions of real family life, I still believe that they conveyed an important truth: children are a blessing. Because we live in a society where children have become optional and therefore easily discarded or at least taken for granted, we must practice remembering the blessing we have in being given little ones.

As excited as we are about our pregnancy, we still occasionally slip into the self-centered thinking promoted by our culture. We worry about how the children will interfere with the allocations in *our* budget, the layout of *our* house, and the scheduling of *our* time. It's easy to miss this basic truth from the Scriptures: Children are a blessing from the Lord!

We are privileged to become parents; children are not a burden but a gift. Whenever we feel stifled by the upcoming changes in our lifestyle, we try to replace the negative attitude with this truth. Instead of saying, "Children are expensive," we say, "Children are a blessing." When our friends warn us that "Children are exhausting," we try to think, "Children are a blessing." While this attitude may not help to pay the bills or locate extra energy, thinking this way helps us joyfully cope with our situation.

God, we rejoice in your gift of little ones. Kindle in us an understanding of how blessed we are.

THE DISCIPLINE OF BELOVED CHILDREN

HEBREWS 12:5–11

And you have forgotten that word of encouragement that addresses you as sons: "My son, do not make light of the Lord's discipline, and do not lose heart when he rebukes you, because the Lord disciplines those he loves, and he punishes everyone he accepts as a son" (vv. 5–6).

We have started attending a parenting class at church on Sunday evenings. We realize we may be a little premature since our children haven't even been born, but we figure if we start now, we'll be better prepared to handle the challenges ahead of us. As we listen to parents discuss the "terrible twos" and "fiercely independent fours" (not to mention the "traumatic teens"), we are overwhelmed by the hard work of helping little ones grow into responsible adulthood. When we were a childless couple, we always had answers when it came to the proper discipline of children, but as real parents we imagine that actually applying our lofty, untried principles will be much more difficult.

Discipline may not be what readily comes to mind when we daydream about becoming parents. It is so much easier to think about cradling a tiny innocent newborn in our arms and counting fingers and toes. Yet we know that discipline is a major part of parenting. If we love our children, we will give them limits to protect them and to teach them. Many people equate discipline with punishment, but the word "discipline" means essentially "to teach." When we discipline children, we teach them values, self-control, and respect for others; we train them to care about whatever we think is important, to choose appropriate behavior regardless of feelings, and to show love to others.

The manner in which we discipline our children will affect the way they view God. If they learn to accept our discipline as an act of love, they will likewise see their heavenly Father's chastening as a sign of his great love for them. Our failure to express our love for our children through disciplining them will lead them to a life of insecurity and mediocrity, at best, and it may even interfere with their ability to accept God's authority over their lives.

Even though we may not have to worry about dispensing consequences for inappropriate behavior to our babies for quite some time yet, we can begin to be prepared, so that we can be proactive rather than reactive in our discipline when the time comes. We can seek to make our approach to discipline a channel through which we can communicate our love to our children, just as God demonstrates his love for us through his chastening.

Father, thank you for your discipline that is evidence of your love for us. Grant us the wisdom to work together as we lovingly discipline our children in every aspect of their lives.

WHAT DO YOU WANT THEM TO BE?

> ISAIAH 6:1–8
> *Then I heard the voice of the LORD saying, "Whom shall I send? And who will go for us?" And I said, "Here am I. Send me!" (v. 8).*

A six-year-old was asked what he wanted to be when he grew up; he joyously replied, "A monkey!" Much to his parents' relief, he grew up to be a safety engineer instead. My parents thought I would be an engineer since I was always taking things apart and reading electronics manuals; now I'm an English teacher. You never know, do you?

Do you already find yourself wondering what career your little one will pursue? Perhaps you see those long fingers on the sonogram and imagine a concert pianist; maybe those painful kicks are coming from a future professional soccer player. It's easy to imagine your child growing up to be a doctor who finds a cure for cancer or following in your footsteps, pursuing your chosen vocation. Few expectant parents would dream of their unborn child's being an inner-city social worker or a missionary in Myanmar.

As parents-to-be, we harbor any number of "visions" for what we want our children to be as adults. That's part of the excitement of having these little bundles of potential and watching them grow up. Our children have the opportunity, perhaps, to be what we are not able to be.

Parents, intentionally or not, set the tone for career explorations. We plant seeds ("fingers like a concert pianist") and set expectations ("kicks like a hammer") before the child is even born. I suppose that the parents of successful children view their children as visible proof of good parenting. However, what could be more rewarding than knowing that your children have sought after and earnestly followed God's calling in their lives? As parents, we must encourage our children to cultivate their gifts and talents as they seek God's calling. We must also instill in them a healthy view of work as a part of God's intended purpose in our lives.

Isaiah heard the call of God and answered immediately. He was willing to follow God's call, to share the message of love with Israel. Many people incorrectly think that the call of God extends only to professional ministry positions, but God's power is not limited to any one vocation. I believe that God called me to serve as a teacher, where I have the opportunity to live my faith in the plain view of students who are struggling with their own faith. I have friends who believe that they were called to be business leaders, mechanics, and homemakers. God desires for all believers to allow him to work through them to share the Good News of Christ while at work. When we view work as God's command and our jobs as God's provision for us, we can accomplish much in his name. As parents, we set the tone for this sense of service.

God, you have called us to faithful service, no matter what our jobs may be. Guide us as we help our children to listen for your calling in their lives.

TOUCHSTONE MOMENTS

> JOSHUA 4:1–3,
> 19–24
>
> *He said to the Israelites,
> "In the future when
> your descendants ask
> their fathers, 'What do
> these stones mean?' tell
> them, 'Israel crossed
> the Jordan on dry
> ground'" (vv. 21–22).*

When we tell our friends that we are having babies, most of my childhood friends immediately make the comment, "Don't you hope they don't have Gene's temper?" That temper was infamous while I was in high school; once I was ejected from a softball game for throwing a bat at an umpire. Most of my friends, however, who didn't know me then would find it hard to believe that I ever had a problem with my temper. I thank God for teaching me how to let his peace saturate me and cool the anger that once ruled so much of my life.

The other day, while moving boxes from the nursery to the garage for storage, I came across my old poster of Monet's painting of the lilies at Giverny. Its caption reads, "Let everything about you breathe the calm and peace of the soul." I bought the poster when God was teaching me to control my temper. I've saved it all these years because it reminds me of how God is molding me into the person he wants me to be.

When I looked at that poster in my garage, I realized that my children may need an object lesson in peaceful living one day. Someday, at an appropriate moment, I will bring out that poster and it will provide me with a touchstone through which I can communicate an important lesson about God's work in my life.

God himself ordained Joshua's use of touchstones. The Israelites understood these stones' lasting value, using them for many generations to pass down the story of God's wondrous actions in their history. Scattered about our offices and homes are many such touchstones: photo albums, scrapbooks, and memorabilia that will provide us with teachable moments wherein we can share our faith, our values, and our heritage.

God, remind us of our touchstone events, and help us to find ways to communicate their important truths to our little ones. Help us to be articulate, especially as we tell them of your love and your plans for their lives.

FUTURE MATES

GENESIS 24:58
*So they called
Rebekah and asked
her, "Will you go
with this man?" "I
will go," she said.*

My parents prayed for my future mate, not just during the teen years, but even before I was born. Somehow I took comfort in that knowledge when I began to wonder if I would ever get married; if Mom's been praying about it, I figured, then it will happen. I thank God for bringing Lisa and me together at just the right time.

We both have clear memories of the first time we met; we were getting tests for tuberculosis! Actually, our paths had crossed many times before that day. For example, we had been to the same church but had never met. I even went to college with Lisa's cousin, yet we had never met. Our parents had literally dozens of friends in common, and still we had not met until that day at orientation for new school teachers (for whom the state required TB tests). The timing, we suppose, had just not been right before then. When we did meet, our hearts melted, and we were married eighteen months later. Now we are expecting twins just after our ninth anniversary.

When we read Genesis 24, we are struck by the divine intervention in the servant's finding Rebekah. Evidently it was the right time for Isaac and Rebekah to meet and to marry. God brought them together for his purposes and on his time schedule. This man and woman were both sensitive to God's plan for their lives, and God used them because of their willingness.

Now the cycle has come around, and it's our turn to be the parents who are praying for this important aspect of our little ones' lives. We want our children to be loved and respected, to have mates who will encourage them both emotionally and spiritually. We want them to have spouses who will love them even more, perhaps, than we do. We want for them to be in God's will and in God's time as they grow into adulthood and begin to contemplate this step in life. We pray, even now, for our children and their future mates.

God, lead our little ones to the right spouse. Help them and their future mates to be patient, pure, and ready at the proper time to make that commitment that is second only to their commitment to Christ.

PREPARATIONS

FORTY WEEKS OF PREPARATION

At first, the news of pregnancy is like manna from heaven, a delight to the heart. As any mother can tell you, though, being pregnant, like eating manna, gets a little old after forty weeks (give or take a couple of weeks). For a baby, the time allotment is just right—just enough time to grow lungs and bones and muscles and all of the other necessary parts and get them working before trying them out in the world, but not so much time that the womb looks too attractive to leave. For parents, the time can seem like it will never end, especially as the due date approaches. Many of our friends have warned Lisa that she will reach a stage where she will find herself saying, "I can't stand to be pregnant one more day!"

In the Scriptures, "forty" often symbolizes testing and preparation. Noah waited for God to cleanse the earth of the unrighteous with a forty-day rainstorm. Moses spent forty days and nights on the mountain preparing to lead the Israelites. God prepared the Israelites to enter Canaan by leading them around the desert for forty years. Elijah traveled forty days and nights to reach the mountain of God. Likewise, Jesus was tested forty days in the wilderness.

We are struck by the symbolic parallel between our forty weeks of pregnancy and God's use of forty days/years in the lives of these biblical characters. Surely, forty days of rain was about all Noah could take, and forty years in the desert must have seemed like an eternity to the Israelites. Yet God deemed that this was the right amount of time for preparing Noah to restore the earth and for the Israelites to become a nation of God's people. Likewise, our Creator's design for parents is perfect, providing baby, mother, and father a perfect window of time to prepare physically, emotionally, financially, and spiritually.

Lord, help us to use the remainder of our pregnancy wisely as we prepare for the arrival of our gift from heaven. Help us not to become discouraged and impatient when the ailments and stresses of pregnancy seem a lot like a walk through the wilderness. Give us the strength to make the journey to the border of Canaan and beyond.

DREAM HOUSES

What does your dream house look like? Perhaps you have a picture in your minds or clippings from magazines. You may have money set aside in your budget for a down payment, a room addition, or maybe new furniture. Many couples who are adding to their families are simultaneously trying to buy, build, or remodel a home. Last year, we bought our first house, a twenty-year-old fixer-upper in need of some major cosmetic surgery. We have used lots of elbow grease on weekends and holidays, replacing ancient shag carpet, laying hardwood floors and tile, refurbishing our front entry, and painting nearly every room in the house. We now know how all-consuming and highly stressful it can be to make a house match our dreams! Put that stress together with the anxieties of having a baby and working at careers, and there isn't much time or energy left for anything else.

In all of the busyness that burdens pregnancy, it's very easy to get distracted from the serious business of building our family life. A real danger at this stage of our lives is that we will spend all our efforts building houses and growing our families, only to realize later that we have left God out of our plans. We may have consulted experts and manuals until we think we know everything ourselves, but this verse reminds us that unless we follow God's Word and consult with the

Master Carpenter, all our labor is in vain. We may end up with a nice house, but not a warm home. God can be the designer and builder of a home beyond our wildest dreams if we make him Lord of our families. If we start now, before the arrival of this new child, we will be better prepared when our family is enlarged.

God, help us to make you Lord of every endeavor, from building a house to having a baby. Give us a vision of what your dream home for us is.

TAKING CARE OF YOURSELVES

> DANIEL 1:3–20
>
> *But Daniel resolved not to defile himself with the royal food and wine, and he asked the chief official for permission not to defile himself this way*
> *(v. 8).*

Gene has found himself going to the fitness center more often these days. He doesn't want to be a fat and lazy old man who can't throw a ball or play tennis with his kids. I am buying healthier foods at the grocery store because I want these babies to get all of the good nutrition they can. Even our parents have taken up this self-improvement mentality so they can be active grandparents who take their grandchildren on "adventures" like the zoo and the beach.

We want our little ones to be healthy, and we want them to have healthy, active parents. Though we have always known that God wants us to treat our bodies as temples, our willpower has succumbed to the pressures of holidays, gluttony, and a lack of self-control. Our unborn children have given us even more incentive to attempt these wise lifestyle changes.

Daniel and his friends made a choice to stay true to their strict diets in a culture in which everyone was eating, drinking, and being merry. It must have taken a lot of willpower on their parts not to indulge, but they resisted and were obviously healthier. They reflected healthy priorities that put God first and their physical appetites much further down the list, actually allowing them to witness to those who were watching how these young men handled this situation. In our age, we know so much about healthy lifestyles, we have no excuse not to be examples for our children. If we start them out right, perhaps they won't have to work so hard at changing unhealthy habits later.

Lord, give us the willpower we need to take better care of ourselves and our little ones. Help us to remember to treat our bodies as living temples of your Spirit.

WHAT'S IN A NAME?

LUKE 1:57–80
*They were going to
name him after his
father Zechariah, but
his mother spoke up
and said, "No! He is
to be called John"*
(vv. 59–60).

Have you decided on any names yet?" We are starting to dread that question. Naming a child is a big responsibility! How do we pick out names? Rule out old boyfriends and girlfriends. Eliminate bosses and supervisors. Drop the name of the strange kid who ate paste in first grade. Suppress the urge to go with Ella for our girl. (Ella Fant? Just imagine the teasing on field trips to the zoo!) Family names? The good ones are taken. What about biblical names: Jerub-Baal, Jezebel, Mephibosheth, and Tubal-Cain? Okay, so those may not work.

We have several of those fancy baby-name books. A suggestion that most of them make is that parents consult the meaning of the names. For instance, my name, "Gene Fant," means, loosely, "Lucky Dude"; "Lisa" means "Consecrated to God." Names can provide a sense of the parents' hopes for their children. What on earth did the parents who named a kid "Turnipseed" (a real name, believe it or not!) hope for?

Though we haven't settled on names yet, we have decided, like Zechariah, to keep the names secret until the babies are born. It's a scene we play over and over again in our minds, their dad carrying the precious little bundles out to the waiting area and introducing them to their relatives.

We want to pick out good names, distinct indicators of what we want to instill in our children: pride and purpose. Certainly, Elizabeth and Zechariah recognized the significance of their son's name. (John means "God is gracious.") Surely they told their little boy from the beginning how special he was; his name was just a start.

Father, you know the importance of names. Help us to pick names that "fit" and that give our babies a sense of how special they are.

INFORMATION OVERLOAD

When we found out that Lisa was pregnant, she eagerly rushed to the store to purchase one of those pregnancy manuals depicting all of the wonderful things that would happen over the next nine months. We pored over this book, hungry for any information we could get to help us understand this uncharted territory. We hunted for pictures of babies at the same stage of development as our little ones. Both of us wanted to know *everything* about what was going on. We felt that with more information, we would be better prepared parents.

Everyone seemed ready to provide us free materials. From our first doctor's visit on, we were given packets and pamphlets. We attended classes on pregnancy health, childbirth, child safety, and breastfeeding, bringing home a library of materials from each. Literature continues to flood our mailbox from formula companies, toy manufacturers, hospitals, insurance companies, and state agencies. Suddenly, we have reached information overload. Indeed, at this moment, we couldn't digest another piece of information about our upcoming event if we had to!

Although much of the information for expectant parents is helpful, little is available to help parents prepare themselves spiritually for this life-changing event. It's easy to focus on gaining knowledge about pregnancy and fetal development while ignoring the profound wisdom necessary for parenting that comes from an intimate relationship with our heavenly Father, the Creator of this new life and our family unit. Perhaps we can spend time talking about our relationships with each other and with God. Maybe we can find ways to pray for and with one another as well as read Scripture together. Above all, we can devote ourselves to being dedicated parents who will equip their children both materially and spiritually.

Father, help us to be wise parents and not simply knowledgeable ones. Remind us that your wisdom far exceeds that of this world, and that we should seek out your leadership in our lives.

DEADLINES

LUKE 10:38–42
*Mary has chosen
what is better, and it
will not be taken
away from her
(v. 42).*

I hate deadlines, but I sure am thankful for them. As a student, I dreaded those upcoming due dates for papers and projects. Each semester, I would always resolve to be better organized, to start projects earlier, and to finish papers ahead of time so that I wouldn't have to be stressed out as the due date approached. No matter how well I planned or how hard I tried to complete assignments ahead of time, I would always find myself working on them late the night before (or the morning) they were due. It seemed that the more time I had, the more I used. I could always think of one more idea I wanted to add or one more change I wanted to make. Whether my paper was ready or not, however, the deadline arrived, and I had to move on. As English teachers, Gene and I have a saying, "There are no finished papers, just ones turned in."

This week, I'm spending my days sitting at an arm's-length distance from my sewing machine because my tummy prevents me from getting any closer. I'm diligently sewing drapes, bumpers, and dust ruffles. (A video of me crawling around on the floor, measuring and cutting out pattern pieces, would have won $10,000 on one of those home video shows.) I wonder if I'll finish before the babies come and, even if I do, I'm sure I'll think of six more projects I'd like to complete before they arrive.

My wise mother-in-law really has a way of putting deadlines into perspective. When we were panic-stricken over finishing wedding preparations, she said, "Just remember, whether you get everything done or not, when the day arrives, you will still be married!" Regardless of our stress over all the preparations for the wedding, the important thing would happen: the marriage would take place. With the preparations for the babies, she has continued to remind us of what's really important: "When those babies are ready to come, they'll come whether you're ready or not. As long as you've got diapers, you'll survive. You can always send someone to Wal-Mart to pick out what's really necessary." She's right. Preparation is important, but it is not what's most important.

The marriage bond and the birth of two new lives are the essentials. Relationships always take priority over tasks. Martha missed out on a blessing because she became bogged down in the preparations; Mary enjoyed the company of Jesus. The details of Martha's hospitable deeds would probably not be remembered, but the time spent at the Master's knee would be precious to Mary for all her life. By nature, I am a Martha type, but pregnancy is teaching me to relax some of my unrealistic standards. Like Mary, I constantly need to evaluate what is good and what is better, refusing to allow preparations to overshadow blessings.

God, teach us to keep our preparations in perspective. Focus our attention on the priorities that truly matter.

DO WE HAVE TO THINK ABOUT THIS?

JOHN 19:25–27
Near the cross of Jesus stood his mother, his mother's sister, Mary the wife of Clopas, and Mary Magdalene. When Jesus saw his mother there, and the disciple whom he loved standing nearby, he said to his mother, "Dear woman, here is your son," and to the disciple, "Here is your mother." From that time on, this disciple took her into his home.

As we write this, we have on our to-do list a number of difficult items: our will, our insurance coverage and beneficiaries, and the custodianship of the children. These issues have been on our list for some time, and we have not dealt with them, partly because we are busy and partly because they are the kinds of issues that we tend to put off. We must make lists of policies and accounts, assets and debts. We need to be responsible adults and plan for unforeseen future events; we should leave things tidy, just in case.

Imagine the thoughts that went through Christ's mind that day as he looked down on his mother and felt the responsibility of a son for his widowed mother who would be left behind. Christ chose his most beloved disciple, probably John himself. He knew that John would treat his mother as his own and would care for her.

How on earth do we make a decision about who can best care for our children should we meet an untimely death or incapacitation? We have so many relatives who would make great foster parents. They would instill our values in our children and teach them to serve God. They would let our little ones know how much we loved them and cared for them. The decision is excruciating. Now is the time, though, to think and pray about this issue. We really do have to talk about such things.

God, our wisdom is weak and flawed. Help us to make the best decisions about our children's care, especially the what-if's of estate planning and custodianship.

FOUNDATIONS
OF FAITH

GOD'S GLORY

PSALM 19:1–2
*The heavens declare
the glory of God; the
skies proclaim the
work of his hands.
Day after day they
pour forth speech;
night after night they
display knowledge.*

When I was a child, I used to love to take a sleeping bag into the yard on warm summer evenings and stretch out on my back. We lived out in the country, where the lack of artificial light made the sky shimmer with starlight. I became an amateur astronomer, reading about astronomy and learning the names of the constellations so that I could identify them.

I suspect that my affinity to stargazing had something to do with my grandfather. He was abandoned by his parents when he was eight or nine, and as a child he was prone to fits of depression and self-doubt. Many times, he told me, he would sit out on a log in the woods, look at the stars, and become overwhelmingly convinced that there must be a God who loves even an unwanted little boy. He never articulated to me exactly what caused this conviction for him, but for him the message of God's love was written in the sky itself. As he grew into adulthood, he always returned to the declaration of creation as evidence of God's care for him.

Tonight as I took out the garbage, I looked up into the bright night sky and saw the nearly full moon and the stars. The air was cool, the wind still. No traffic could be heard; I was aware of my own breathing. Overcome with a sense of the beauty of creation, I lingered there for several moments, thinking about the majesty of God. I also remembered my grandfather's story of God's love.

I guess that impending fatherhood has made me sensitive to these things, but the thought occurred to me that soon I will stand under the night sky with a baby in my arms! I can show my very own flesh and blood the stars and their con- stellations. I can talk about the Creator of the heavens who loves each of us so much that he gave his own life for us. When God's very creation cries out in testimony of his majesty, can I be silent?

God, you are the Creator and Lord of the universe. Give us all listening ears and willing mouths for the testimony of your glories.

TREASURES

LUKE 2:1–20
But Mary treasured up all these things and pondered them in her heart (v. 19).

Pregnancy and birth are wondrous events tucked into our ordinary lives. Realizing the significance of bringing a new life into the world, most couples try to preserve their memories of this marvelous time. We can't wait to capture and preserve every important moment with our new camcorder. Gene isn't allowed to tape the birth itself, but we want a video record of the baby's every smile, grimace, coo, and cry.

What is the value of storing up these memories? Certainly Mary took time to reflect on her situation as the mother of Christ. She soaked in all of the incredible events that surrounded her firstborn's birth and growth into adulthood. She must have thought often about the events that are described in Luke 2: the coming of the shepherds and angels, the adoration of the baby by Simeon and Anna, and the family visit to the temple when Jesus dazzled the scholars with his intelligence. Perhaps her memories helped to sustain her through the pain of his death. She had laid up treasures by watching, thinking about, and pondering the events of her days as a young mother.

Pregnancy is not an everyday experience; for most couples, it will happen only a few times. We have begun storing up our memories and, by doing so, we are already bonding with our baby. Once he or she arrives, each day that we have together will be a day to make memories and to store up treasures. Once past, a day is lost forever. How important that we give ourselves time to ponder the richness of our lives, discovering God's involvement in our ordinary activities.

God, keep us from being so caught up in the details of living that we miss out on the little miracles occurring in our little one's earliest days.

THE GOSPEL IN THE WOMB

> **LUKE 1:39–45**
> *As soon as the sound of your greeting reached my ears, the baby in my womb leaped for joy (v. 44).*

"Prenatal." How many times a day do you read that term now? We have prenatal vitamins, prenatal nutrition, prenatal workouts, and prenatal checkups. Never before have people been so interested in the development of babies before they are born. We know many couples who are trying to get a head start on their little one's education by speaking French or other languages during the pregnancy. We know others who have put headphones on the baby's ears (mommy's tummy) and played classical music. Lisa's stepmother, a music educator, says that early exposure to music increases children's overall learning abilities.

If we can use music to shape our children's intellectual interests, why not cultivate their spiritual sensitivities as well? We heard of one expectant father who sang "Jesus Loves Me" repeatedly to his pregnant wife's tummy. After the baby was born, in apparent recognition of the song, the child would coo and rock himself every time his dad would sing that song. Because his parents emanated the love of Jesus as they sang, perhaps he even sensed the meaning of the lyrics. His parents had treated him to a prenatal Sunday school!

We have picked three songs to sing over and over to our babies: "Jesus Loves Me," "Jesus Loves the Little Children," and "This Little Light of Mine." We get tickled whenever Lisa feels the children wiggle as we sing these simple songs; perhaps they are "leaping for joy" at the sound of God's message of salvation.

God clearly has some relationship with the child in the womb. David (Ps. 139) knew that God had cared for him while he was still in his mother's womb. Jeremiah (Jer. 1:5) believed that God had planned to use him as a prophet before his parents had even conceived him. John the Baptist (this passage) was spiritually sensitive before he was born. Each of these men was touched in a mysterious way while yet in his mother's womb. We can begin to prepare our little ones' hearts for the deep love of Christ even at this early stage.

Lord, prepare the hearts of our little ones for the message of the Gospel. Attune their ears to your loving words.

GOD'S WORD

> **PSALM 119:11**
> *I have hidden your word in my heart that I might not sin against you.*

As a little boy I was prone to nightmares. Many nights I woke up terrified and sweating; my fears were often compounded by the numerous nighttime thunderstorms we had in the deep South. I still remember the first Bible verse I learned by heart (my parents taught me to repeat it to myself on such occasions), Psalm 56:3 in the old King James: "What time I am afraid, I will trust in thee."

Recently my parents decided to reduce their library, and they let me select books to put in my own personal library. Among those I picked was our family devotional Bible. I have very early memories of sitting around the breakfast table while Dad read. On cold mornings, I used to wrap up in a blanket at the table and sit over the furnace register while I listened. As I reflect on those times, I realize that my heart was being sown with the seeds of God's Word. Even during our pregnancy, when I am overcome with a sense of dread or fear, I find myself repeating that simple verse, "What time I am afraid, I will trust in thee."

We have been talking about how we want to handle a family quiet time with our children. We look forward to lying next to our little ones at bedtime and reading about our favorite Bible heroes. What a thrill to rediscover stories like that of David, the young shepherd boy whom God selected to become king of Israel; how wondrous to renew our awe over the baby in the manger who grew up and gave his life for us.

Family readings in the Bible can become meaningless ritual if we aren't careful. The Bible's stories are not just children's stories meant to be outgrown somewhere along the way. My parents used Psalm 56 to teach me a great lesson: God's Word still works in our lives. We need to learn to apply the message of Scripture as we read it to our children. The evils facing Noah and the temptations confronting David are still ones we face today. Likewise, God's love and care for these people remind us of his love toward us. The story of Christ's birth, death, and resurrection is the good news of the first century as well as of our own century. The Bible's wonderful stories mean little if they are simply quaint stories. Their power comes from their ability to speak to us today, providing us with a compass in our spiritual wilderness.

Living Word, speak to us as we prepare ourselves for the arrival of our little ones. Help us to teach them how to see themselves in the Scriptures and how to listen for your voice.

LOVE OF CHURCH

A few years ago the church we attended had a high-attendance Sunday with a fairly lofty attendance goal. When the count came in, we were only five persons short of the goal. The pastor, without missing a beat, declared the goal met. He wasn't using a "ministerial estimate," he explained. He knew of at least a half-dozen women in the church who were expecting babies and were present. He figured that he was justified in counting those babies in the womb toward our goal!

Because my dad was a church planter in western New York, church was always a family activity for us. For a while, the small church met in our home. My bedroom was the Sunday school room (that's one way to get the perfect attendance award); the den was the church nursery; and the living room was the sanctuary. There was even a baptistery in the garage! Each Saturday our family worked together, vacuuming, cleaning, and setting up chairs to prepare the house for Sunday's activities.

These preparations actually taught me a good lesson about how the love of church begins in the home. As those of you who already have children will attest, it takes a great deal of effort to go to church and to arrive in a spirit that is prepared to worship. In fact, it's hard work! Everyone must participate in the preparations.

There are other activities that would be easier to do on a beautiful Sunday. As we drive to church, we see families who are using their Sundays for soccer matches and softball games. How sad that these children won't have the experience of attending church with their families! We feel the weighty responsibility of cultivating our children's love of God's house; in a way, we feel that our children are already going to church with us. When the four of us (including the two little ones still in the womb) sit in the pew together at church, we are already worshiping as a family. We hope our children will continue to find it a joy when Sundays roll around and it is time to go into the house of the Lord.

Father, we love visiting your house and worshiping you. Help our little ones to develop a sense of how privileged we are to worship you.

FUTURE PASTORS AND RELIGIOUS TEACHERS

> **EPHESIANS 4:11–13**
>
> *It was he who gave some to be apostles, some to be prophets, some to be evangelists, and some to be pastors and teachers, to prepare God's people for works of service, so that the body of Christ may be built up until we all reach unity in the faith and in the knowledge of the Son of God and become mature, attaining to the whole measure of the fullness of Christ.*

We just met with all the other expectant couples in our church. The preschool minister, Angie, assembled us to talk about the excellent child-care programs that will be offered to our children. She even invited a pediatrician to speak to us about the medical aspects of the church nursery rules and regulations. ("Green runny noses are turned away." We'd never thought about that before!) We learned about the details of our church's baby dedication ceremony. For the first time, we thought seriously about our babies' first pastor and teachers and how important they would be in their lives.

As the meeting concluded, Angie took us on a tour of the facilities. We saw the cribs and the automatic swings, neatly lining the walls. Angie pointed out the posters depicting Jesus, children, church activities, and families, explaining that the preschool teachers teach the little ones lessons even in infancy. We were introduced to our children's first Sunday school teachers.

Who is the first Sunday school teacher you can remember? Mine was my Granny Fant, the sweetest little woman in the world. She smelled of hand cream and lilacs, and she usually wore a red hat to church. I can remember the dark, paneled room where we met to sing songs and make crafts. I remember arguing with her about whether "John the Baptist" had two b's or just one in his name. Most importantly, I remember how her smiles, her hugs, and her constant encouragement of each child in the room taught that small class of children about the love of Christ. Granny taught us the basic truths upon which every other theological truth is built: God loves us; God cares for us; and God wants us to love and care for each other.

Did a special pastor influence your life? Lisa's pastor through her adolescence and young adulthood taught her about the practical application of scriptural principles. From Pastor Turner she learned that being a Christian is not just assuming a title or adopting a set of beliefs but having a relationship with God. She fondly remembers his quirky sayings, songs of yesteryear (which he would sing *a capella* in the middle of his sermons), and anecdotes that so aptly illustrated his points. Lisa particularly remembers his sermons on the family, which continue to influence her as she embarks on her new role as a mother.

The precious pastors and teachers who have ministered to us in official and unofficial ways have led us to mature faith. They embodied the ideals of the Great Commission as they discipled us and taught us to observe the commandments of God. We look forward to seeing how our little ones are influenced by the spiritual leaders in their lives.

God, provide us with dedicated pastors and teachers who will love our little ones. Prepare them to teach our children about your care for each of us.

A PRAYER FOR SALVATION

> ISAIAH 53:4–5
> *Surely he took up our*
> *infirmities and carried*
> *our sorrows, yet we*
> *considered him*
> *stricken by God,*
> *smitten by him, and*
> *afflicted. But he was*
> *pierced for our trans-*
> *gressions, he was*
> *crushed for our iniq-*
> *uities; the punishment*
> *that brought us peace*
> *was upon him, and*
> *by his wounds we*
> *are healed.*

I can't remember what I said, but I'm sure it wasn't the first time I'd said it. I had used some filthy, forbidden expression; my dad had heard me, and we were headed upstairs to the bathroom. I knew what was coming: soap on the toothbrush. My folks still believed in that good old-fashioned remedy for a dirty mouth; I was developing a taste for the French-milled variety.

I can remember Dad sitting me down on the side of the bathtub where I watched him wet a toothbrush in the sink and foam it up with soap. Dad reminded me about the rule for what was probably the twentieth time: foul language had to be cleaned up. I nodded and opened my mouth to accept my bitter punishment.

This time, however, Dad did something different. He told me that Jesus loved me and had died for me. Jesus had never broken the rules, but he took the punishment for everyone's sins. Dad said, "You broke the rules, but I love you so much that I will take your punishment for you. This is just a reminder of what Christ did for you." He brushed his teeth with what I then realized was *his* soap-foamed toothbrush, rinsed his mouth out, and took me to my bedroom, leaving me alone for a few minutes. By the time he returned, my soul was parched with conviction, and I craved relief. I can still remember the coolness of the room and the peace that hung in the air as he led me to pray, and I asked Jesus to be my savior.

My parents had prayed for that moment since before I was born. God had planned for that moment since the creation of the universe. Now Lisa and I pray that there will be teachable moments in our future when our little ones will claim God's offer of salvation.

God, touch the hearts of our little ones and give us opportunities to demonstrate the good news of your love for them.

BIRTH

SAVORING THE PRESENT

> **PSALM 23:2–3**
> *He makes me lie down in green pastures, he leads me beside quiet waters, he restores my soul.*

At this late stage of pregnancy, my doctor has instructed me to take twenty-minute rest breaks every couple hours. Following the collective advice of my physician and other mothers of twins, I prop up my feet, drink a tall glass of water, and then lie down on my left side to increase the blood flow to the placenta. As I recline quietly, my mind drifts to the list of things I need to be doing. Whenever I am tempted to hop up and dust the furniture or run the vacuum, however, I force myself to relish the peacefulness of these moments, knowing that crying babies will soon enough interrupt my rest.

When Beth was nearing her due date, people would say things like, "I bet you're so ready to have that baby" or "I bet you can't wait for the baby to come." She would smile, for their guesses were certainly true, but deep down inside, she was enjoying the way things were. Birth would be the beginning of a new era in her life, but it would also be the end of life as she knew it.

Instead of wishing that her pregnant days were over, she was appreciating time alone with Nick. He had taken her out to an expensive restaurant for her birthday. She savored every moment of romantic solitude, knowing they might not have this opportunity again for a long time. She was also enjoying her own freedom. She could still go to her water aerobics class without packing a diaper bag; she could go out to eat with friends without timing her outing around a baby's schedule; she could go for a walk without taking a stroller. Yes, she looked forward to the birth of her first child with great anticipation and joy, but she knew she would be a more satisfied mom if she also relished the moments she had now.

Living in the present is not a skill we teach our children to do well. We often unwittingly encourage their desire to grow up too fast by focusing exclusively on their futures. We ask them what they want to be when they grow up and tell them they have potential (rather than that they're terrific the way they are now). We tell them to get good grades so they can get into college instead of encouraging learning for the sheer fun of it. The result of all this future thinking is that, by the time we are adults, we have had little training or opportunity to practice resting in the present. Goals are important and we should plan for the future, but not if focusing on future days robs us of the gift of the present.

Whether you are having your first child or not, life will change when this new baby comes. If you cannot enjoy lying down in the green pastures beside still waters now, chances are you won't have the skills to savor precious moments when your baby is born either. God daily gives us many chances for restoring our souls—in a beautiful sunset on our drive home from work or in a spontaneous urge to eat an ice-cream cone with chocolate sprinkles—but we will miss these opportunities if we do not learn to recognize the value of the present.

Lord, teach us to learn from the past, hope for the future, but live in the present. Help us to practice appreciating the richness of our lives, starting now.

GOOD THINGS COME TO THOSE WHO WAIT

Everything is ready. The diaper bag sits next to my packed suitcase. The bassinet has been moved into our bedroom. Stacks of diapers fill the closet in the nursery.

Now we wait.

So much of life is spent waiting. Waiting in traffic, waiting to speak to a real person on the phone, waiting at the doctor's office, waiting in line at the grocery store, waiting to receive grades or test scores or tax refunds. Suspense and thriller movies are popular because they capitalize on our willingness to wait to find out what happens next.

When you were a child, waiting was hard. You had to learn to wait for the cookies to come out of the oven, for summer vacation to arrive, for your birthday party on Saturday. Did you ever peek at your Christmas presents before Christmas? Do you remember how you felt on Christmas morning? The joy of opening your presents was ruined because you had cut short the waiting period.

The natural world taught us about waiting, too. We waited for the robin's eggs in the tree in the front yard to hatch. We watched the terrarium at school, expectantly waiting for the caterpillar we found on the playground to emerge from its cocoon as a butterfly. We waited for the bean seeds we had planted in glass jars to sprout, and then we waited for them to produce beans. We learned valuable lessons about waiting when we impatiently tried to rush these natural processes. The end result of our intervention was always disaster as we scared away the mother bird upon whom those nestlings depended, as we robbed the emergent butterfly of the strength necessary to fly, or as we severed the tender bean sprouts. Have you noticed that chicken just doesn't taste as good since they started trying to speed up the growth process? Shortening the time it takes to make bigger chickens faster has ruined the taste.

I love old things: antique furniture, vintage linens, and historic homes. I admire the craftsmanship of antiques, the attention to detail, the individualized handwork, and the hours lovingly spent creating a thing of beauty.

Often the value of these items is increased by time. I remember how excited Gene's grandfather was when his old Ford truck turned twenty-five, allowing him to order license plates denoting it as a registered antique. It was an ordinary pickup truck when he bought it; now it's a collector's item.

So what gives us the will to wait patiently? It is the hope that we will get something better by waiting. If we hold on to that old dresser, it may be worth something someday. If we wait patiently for the insect to emerge, we may get a glorious glimpse of a brand-new butterfly. If we leave our money in the stock market, we hope we will make more.

In pregnancy, we have little choice about waiting. Waiting is part of the package, but we can deal with the agony of anticipation more easily if we cling to the hope that our waiting is producing a healthy baby. As an expectant mother of twins, I know that the closer we get to the fortieth week of pregnancy before the birth of our babies, the healthier the babies will be.

Pregnancy is a great illustration of God's work in us. Just as he is growing that little child within, he is also growing us, shaping our minds, our characters, our hearts into the perfected children he envisions us to be. It is so easy to become impatient with ourselves, with our imperfections, our habitual sins. We sometimes cannot believe that God doesn't want to give up on us. If we had it our way, we would achieve perfection immediately. (We are, after all, a fast-food generation.) But God is patient, working us over time, not rushing the process, but rather, like a true craftsman, giving attention to every detail, making us better with age. We must be patient with his work in us just as we are patiently awaiting the completed work of our little ones.

Creator, thank you for teaching us through the experiences of life the value of waiting. Help us to be patient as we wait for you to finish your good work in us and on our babies in the womb.

JOY AND PAIN

I walked into my doctor's office for my weekly appointment, expecting to find the nurse putting me through my regular routine: urine speciman, blood pressure, weight check, and an escort to the examining room to wait for the doctor. Instead, I found a woman in obvious pain sitting at the nurse's desk talking on the phone. She was having difficulty making complete sentences.

"Okay. Well, please ... have him call me ... you know, at the doctor's office when he gets in. If I'm not here, I guess I'll be at the [grimace] hospital."

She turned to the nurse. "They can't find him. He's out on the rig, they think. It'll be at least three hours before he gets here even if he could leave right now." After a few comforting words, the nurse walked out to find a place for the woman to lie down.

I stood across the aisle from the woman by the bathroom door, still waiting for instructions. All I could think was, *Wow! She's in labor!* I'd never seen anybody in labor before and, given my present condition, seeing her bent over and clutching the desk was a little unnerving. I really felt sorry for her, especially since it seemed that her husband wouldn't be around for a while. She looked scared. I started to say something, but she put her head on the desk before I could think of anything appropriate.

I was worried. *I don't think I'm ready for this.*

All of us have seen the television sitcoms showing pregnant women giving birth. The husband stands by at the mercy of his wife's labor pains. There's lots of yelling, moaning, sweating, and screaming things like, "Don't you ever touch me again." While we may chuckle at these cartoonish depictions of the birth process, we may also be a little fearful of the grain of truth in these scenes. We all know that birth is painful. In fact, labor is aptly titled because it is exhausting work. As expectant parents, we also know that birth is inevitable.

Although watching videos and practicing our relaxation techniques can go a long way toward helping us feel prepared, as the due date approaches, both husband and wife naturally may become increasingly apprehensive about labor and delivery. A woman may worry about the pain of labor and her ability to persevere through the delivery, while her husband may be concerned about the safety of his wife and child.

Just as we all know birth is painful, we also know that the joy of bringing a child into the world overshadows the pain. (The sitcom writers have that part right.) Jesus could use the experience of birth as an illustration only because everyone understood the truth of his analogy. The mixture of pain and joy in the birth process was an illustration that should have given the disciples hope that Jesus' imminent death was just a sign of the imminent joy that would follow. He would return, giving cause for great rejoicing.

In our modern world in which painkillers are so easily obtained, we may lose some of the lesson God intended in the connection between joy and pain. Joy is multiplied when suffering has preceded it. If you've ever been in acute pain from a migraine, a broken bone, a kidney stone, or a condition more serious, you know the exhilaration of finally being released from that pain. You know the joy of being pain-free, although you may have previously taken the absence of suffering for granted.

I've always found the verse that pronounces the curse on Eve (Gen. 3:16) to be intriguing. The verse states that the woman's labor pains will be greatly *increased*. Perhaps God has always intended for there to be some pain in the birth process. Any creative process is to some degree painful. When I was writing my master's thesis, I jokingly said that it took me nine months to write and the process was just as painful as birth. Making a dream come true almost always requires travail. The suffering we endure only serves to increase our joy at the accomplishment.

God, thank you for the gift of pain that strengthens and refines us. Help us through the painful moments to focus on the joy ahead of us.

ENDURANCE

ISAIAH
40:28–31
*Do you not know?
Have you not heard?
The LORD is the ever-
lasting God, the
Creator of the ends of
the earth. He will not
grow tired or
weary. ... but those
who hope in the
LORD will renew their
strength. They will
soar on wings like
eagles; they will run
and not grow weary,
they will walk and
not be faint
(vv. 28, 31).*

We had a meeting with a child-birth educator to teach us how to care for umbilical stumps, circumcisions, cradle cap, and other newborn matters. It was an informative meeting, as neither of us had ever dealt with these issues before. After a while, though, I found the session overwhelming and even a bit boring. I kept yawning and I wondered, *Why on earth did we schedule this during my power nap time?*

Nap time? If I can't stay awake after missing only my afternoon nap, how will I survive weeks of sleep deprivation after our babies arrive?

Babies are exhausting. Have you seen bleary-eyed friends with newborns? Have you heard their descriptions of what the first few weeks are like? One mother told us that her nerves finally reached the breaking point one night about 3 A.M. when she had to hold down a sobbing, thrashing baby while her husband took the baby's temperature rectally. Added to such incidents is the pressure of having visitors dropping by to "ooh" and "aah" over the new arrival. How will we be able to handle all of these tasks when we are so completely worn out?

We are worried about how we will handle those first few weeks. Lisa doesn't function well without sleep. I'm concerned about being coherent at work after staying up all night. Even parents who have had children before do not know how the new baby will be different or how to handle a toddler *and* a newborn. This Scripture promises us that our Creator will renew our strength and provide us with the endurance we need to get through the weary days ahead.

God, give us strength and perseverance as we learn how to care for our little ones. Help us to realize that even those difficult days will pass quickly.

THE ROAD TO DELIVERY

PROVERBS 3:5–6
*Trust in the LORD
with all your heart
and lean not on your
own understanding;
in all your ways
acknowledge him,
and he will make
your paths straight.*

Every Sunday on our way to church, we drive by the hospital where we will be going in a few weeks for the delivery of the babies. As we pass the building, Lisa will pat her tummy and say, "You guys are going to be over there soon! We can't wait to see you."

The ten-mile trip to the hospital is bumpy, has numerous construction zones, and requires several turns across traffic at major intersections. These Sunday morning trips do double duty: they get us to church, and they allow us to practice our routes to the hospital emergency room. We know every light cycle, every intersection, every firehouse along the way (for help in an emergency if we can't reach the hospital fast enough), and every possible alternative route.

We don't believe the childbirth educators who tell us we'll have plenty of time. We imagine how it will be, Lisa in the throes of labor and me trying not to speed or run red lights. Above all else, we are planning for the unknown, but we are praying for a straight route (no wrecks, no construction delays, no unforeseen travel difficulties) when that day arrives.

We have almost arrived at the end of this journey of pregnancy. We have worked through the possibilities, hopes, and fears; the due date is near, and we have found ourselves relying on God's wisdom more each day. We are so weary and joyous at the same time; pregnancy has taught us to acknowledge him as Lord and to trust him with all of our hearts. With these final days upon us, we have realized just how much we truly need and depend on him.

God, lead us in these last few days of pregnancy. Make our ways straight as we depend on you.

DAD'S FINAL THOUGHTS:
The Joy of Birth

> PSALM 136:1
> Give thanks to the
> LORD, for he is good.
> His love endures
> forever.

This morning we went to see our obstetrician, and he told us it was time. He instructed us to meet him at the hospital where he would perform the cesarean section that would bring our little ones into the world. We called our families and headed for the hospital, two weeks before the due date we'd marked on our calendars.

Ironically, the drive over was amazingly quiet. All of our previous practicing of travel routes had been in vain. We traveled to the hospital from the doctor's office, on the other side of town. It's an almost straight route—only one turn a few blocks from the hospital itself. God had indeed made our path straight!

Today is Good Friday; what a special day in my life! At a Good Friday service when I was eight years old, I joined the church with my public profession of faith in Christ. On Good Friday when I was twenty-five, Lisa and I rehearsed for our wedding the next day. Now I would become a dad on Good Friday. The name of this holy day says it all.

I put on my surgical scrubs and scoured my hands. The obstetrics nurse ushered me into the crowded delivery room where Lisa was lying on an operating table. Dr. Ethridge looked at me and says, "Here we go!" Less than a minute later, a chubby little baby boy came out yelling. The next minute, out came his sister with beautiful black hair sticking out all over her head. How amazing it was to see my son, my daughter, and my wife together for the first time.

Less than ten minutes later, the nurses handed me both babies—my children. My little girl looked so delicate, wiggling in her swaddling blanket. My son yelled a bit and looked around alertly. I carried them out to the waiting room and introduced them to their grandparents, their Aunt Tina, and their Great-aunt Jane.

Even now I can hardly recapture the memories, much less the emotions, of that moment. When pregnancy ends so spectacularly, with healthy children and a wife recovering safely, all one can do is say three simple words:

Thank you, God.

MOM'S FINAL THOUGHTS:
The Joy of Birth

> **PROVERBS
> 13:12**
> *Hope deferred makes
> the heart sick, but a
> longing fulfilled is a
> tree of life.*

Today I was admitted to the hospital for the cesarean birth of our twins. As my mom, my sister, Gene's parents, and my husband were gathered in the room, my fears over the delivery faded. I felt nothing but peace and joyful anticipation. While we waited for the nurses to come for me, I asked Gene's dad to pray, and we all joined hands. The fetal monitor registered two little heartbeats under the resonant tones of my father-in-law's voice. God was there.

In the delivery room, I prayed that I would stop shivering long enough for the anesthesiologist to insert the needle into my spine. The nurse brought me a blanket, and I instantly became still again. During the operation, since I couldn't see anything but Gene and the ceiling or feel anything below my waist, the nurses and doctors told me what was happening. In a few short minutes, I heard my little boy crying, telling me that he was alive and well, and tears streamed down my cheeks. Then a tiny girl. "Hold her up so I can see her," I asked. Her little pink body was squirming, dancing to her brother's song. Within minutes, the nurses brought my two little babies, wearing knit caps and swaddled in blankets, with only their tiny faces uncovered, for me to kiss.

Now, as I nurse my little ones for the first time, I think about how long I was heartsick over not being able to conceive, about how I had nearly given up hope. Today my longing was fulfilled. I've done nothing to deserve these gifts; God is gracious.

Our lives are filled with hopes and dreams, some of them fulfilled, some of them deferred. Perhaps somewhere down the road we will pray for our children's salvation or for God's healing of a broken marriage or for physical healing from cancer, and God's answer may be, "Wait." I pray that when my hope begins to flag, I will remember this moment. I know he holds me in his arms, just as I now hold my little ones, and he is faithful to the end.

Father, your faithfulness constantly amazes me. Help me always to trust in your goodness.

REFLECTIONS

REFLECTIONS

REFLECTIONS

REFLECTIONS

REFLECTIONS

REFLECTIONS

REFLECTIONS

REFLECTIONS

We want to hear from you. Please send your comments about
this book to us in care of the address below. Thank you.

ZondervanPublishingHouse
Grand Rapids, Michigan 49530
http://www.zondervan.com